handsom
PHOTO JOURNAL

Copyright © 2019 by Peter Slater
All rights reserved. This book or any portion thereof
may not be reproduced or used in any manner whatsoever
without the express written permission of the publisher
except for the use of brief quotations in a book review.
Printed in the United States of America

FOR THE
MEN IN MY
LIFE

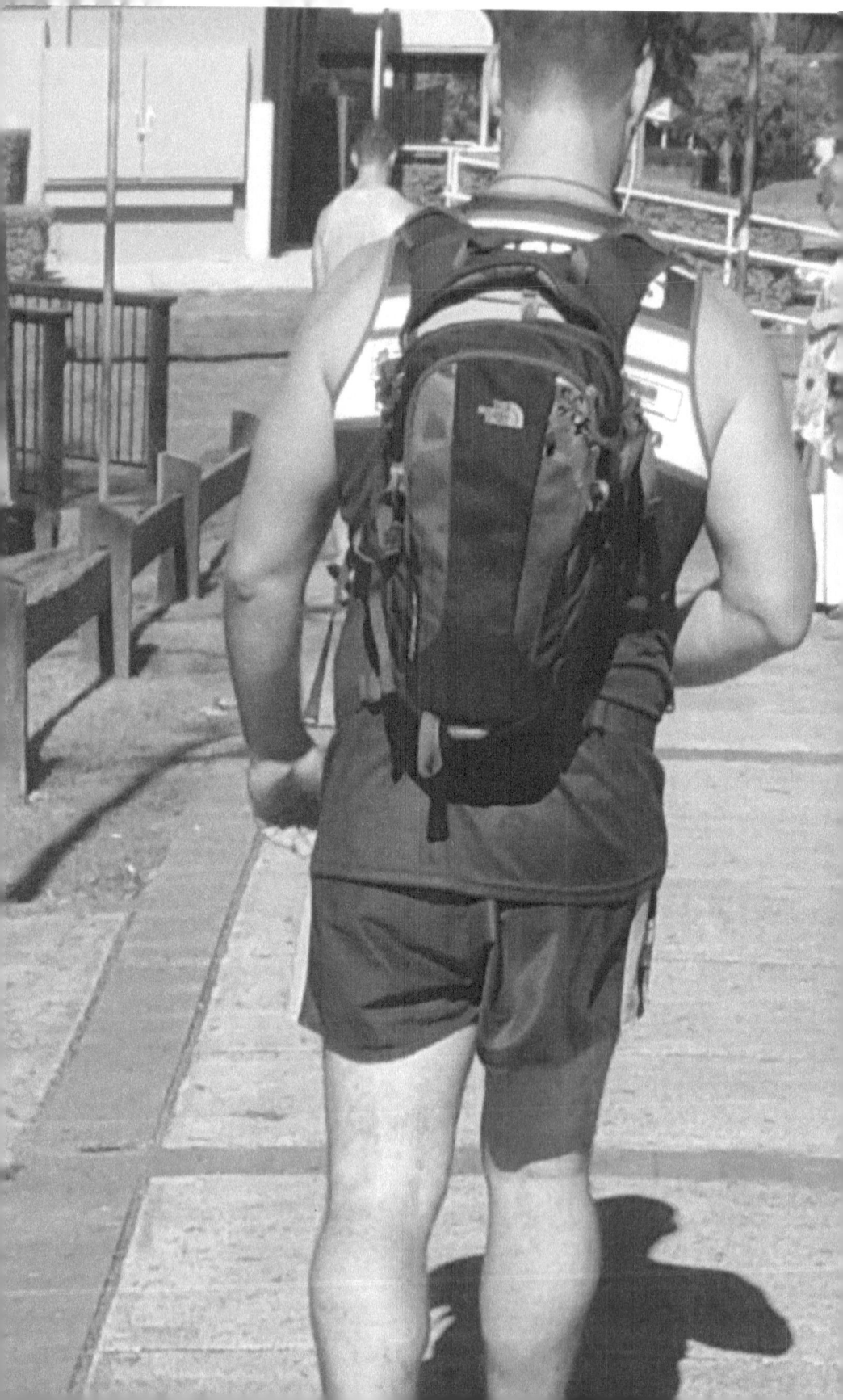

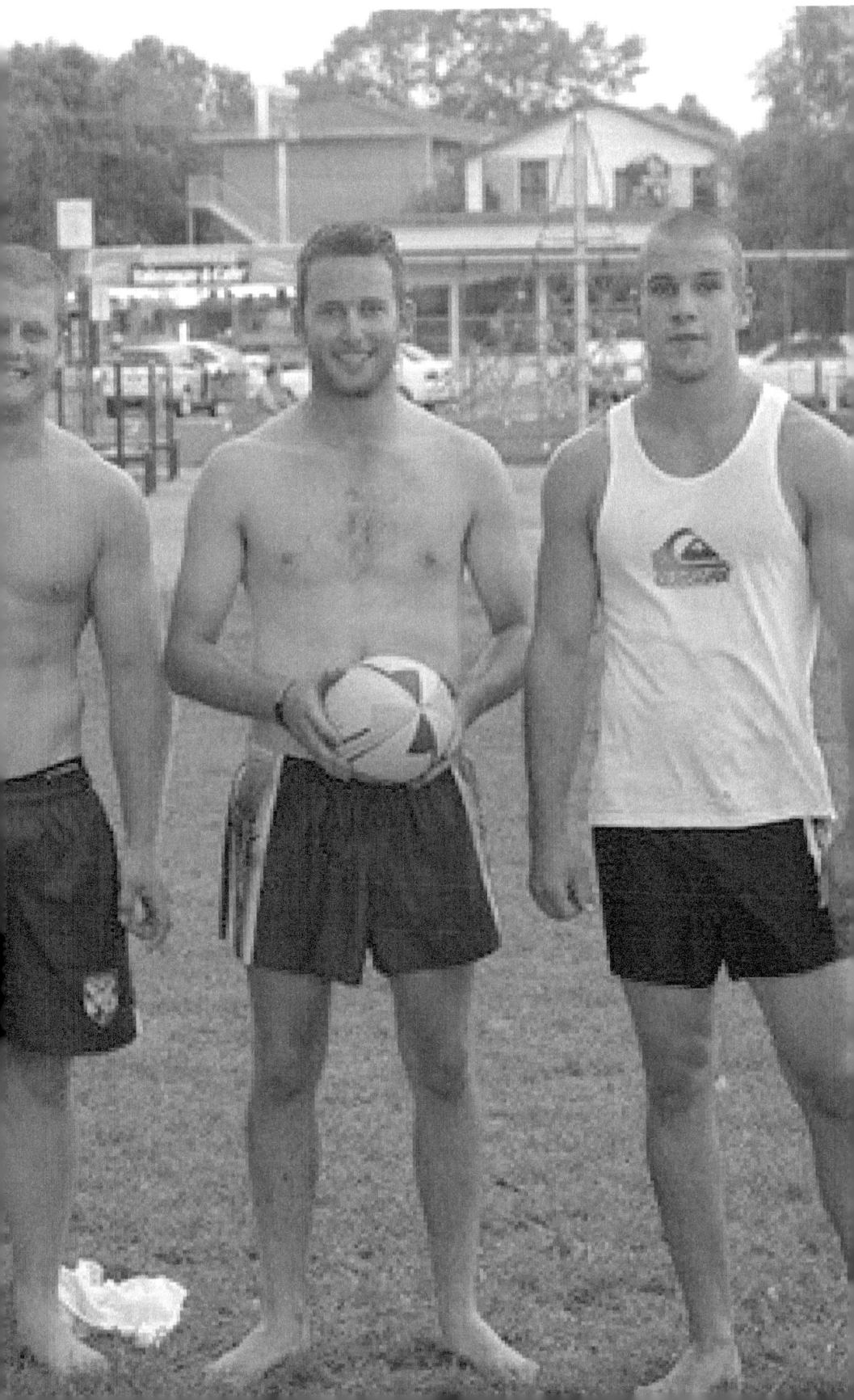

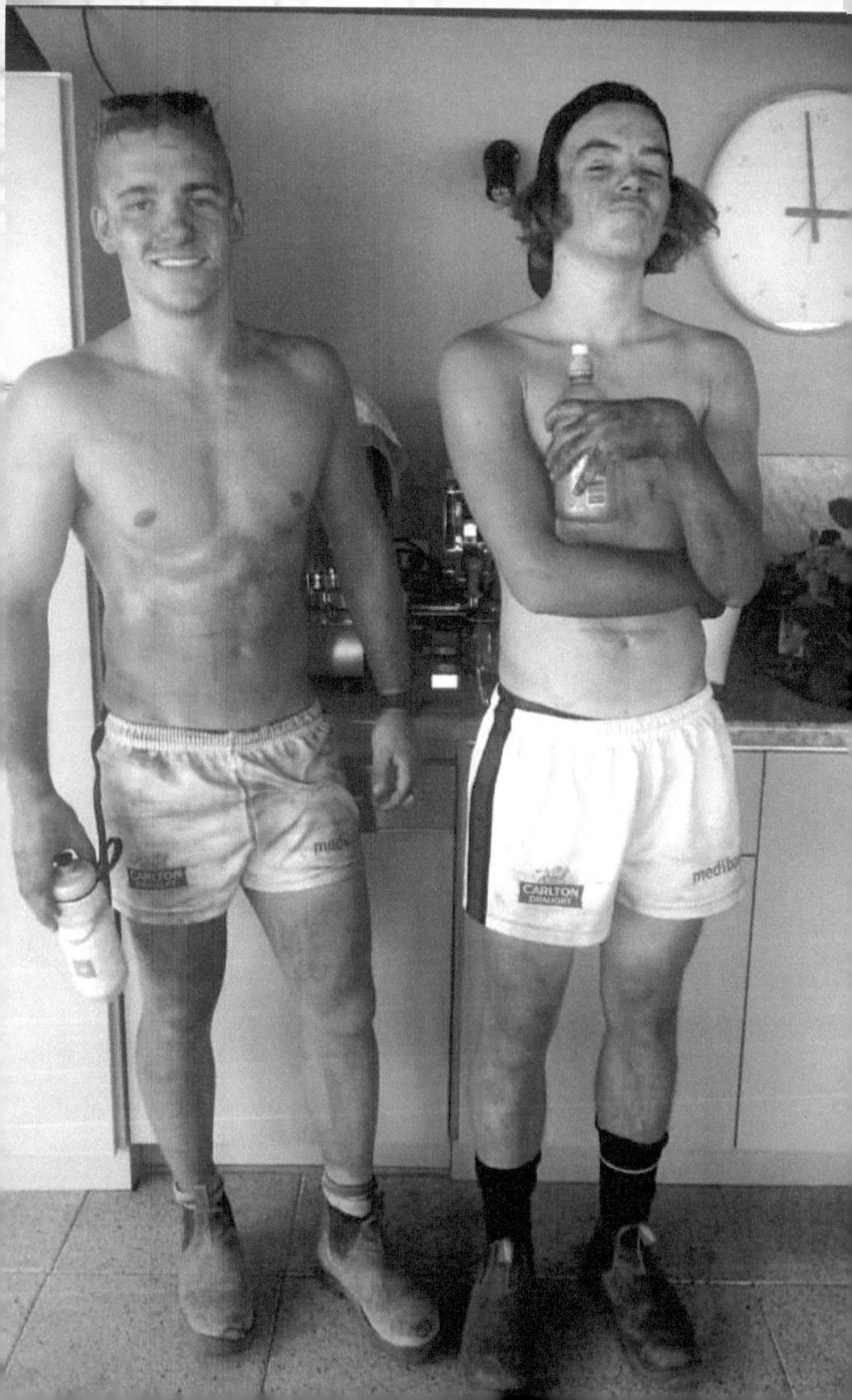

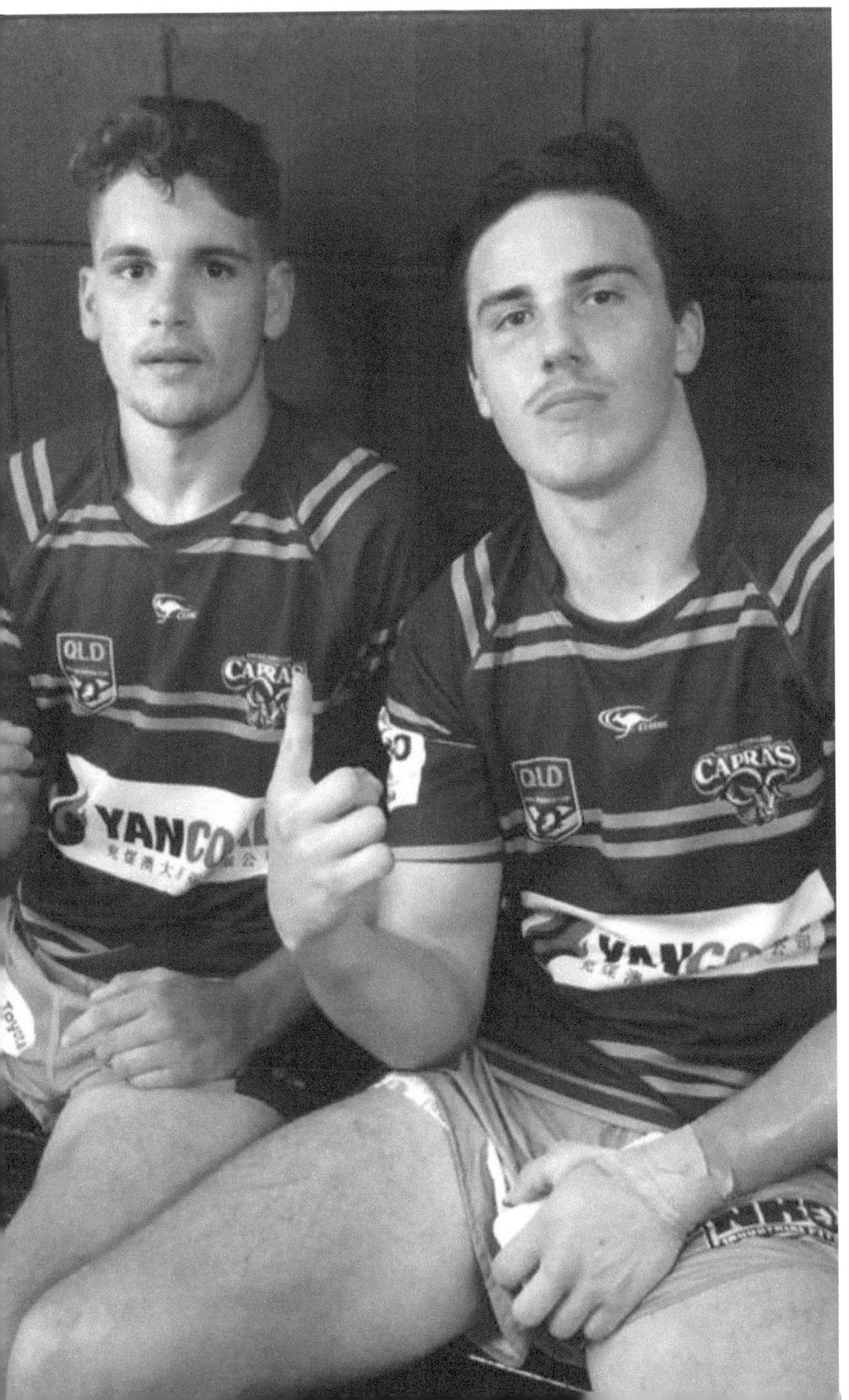

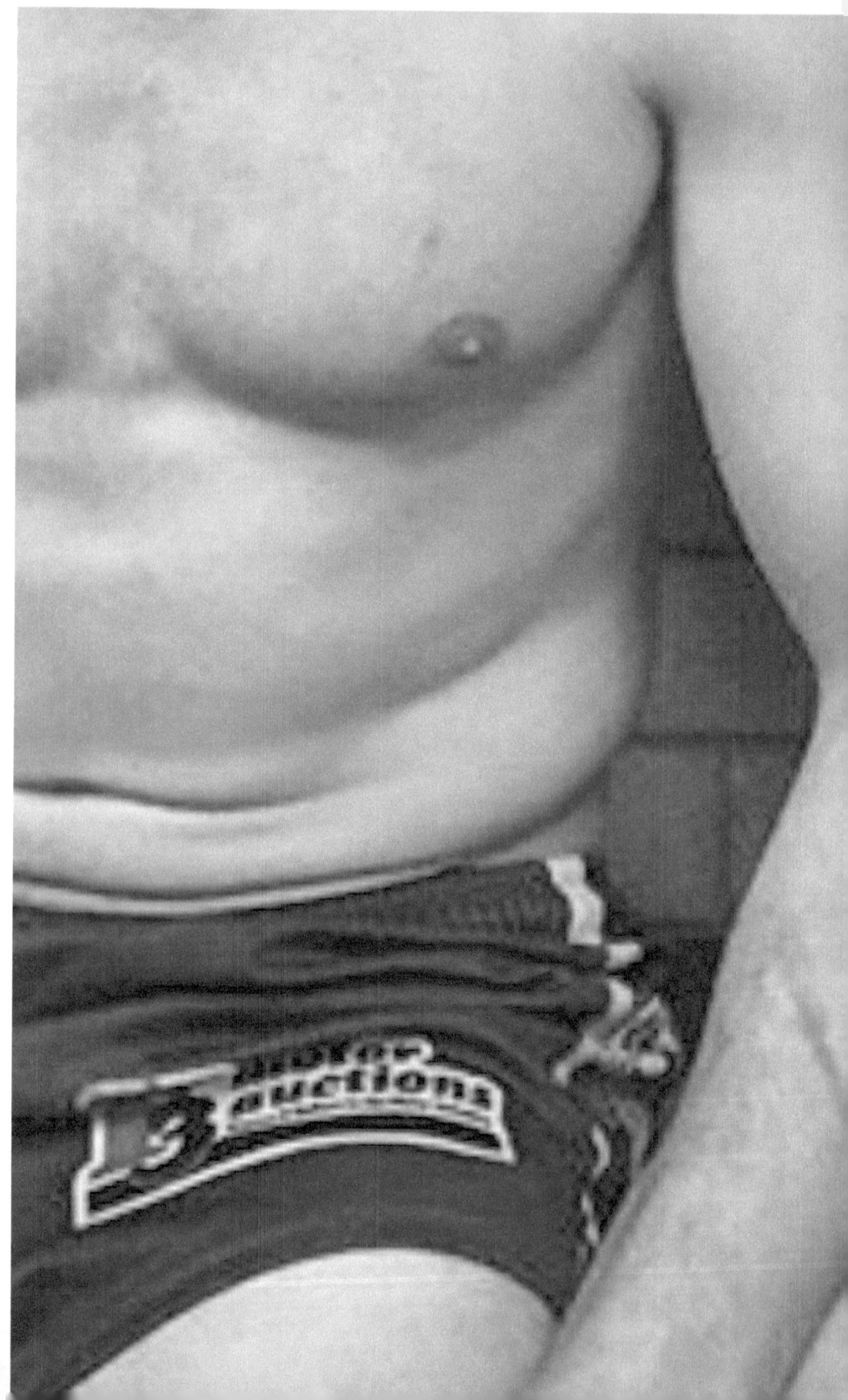

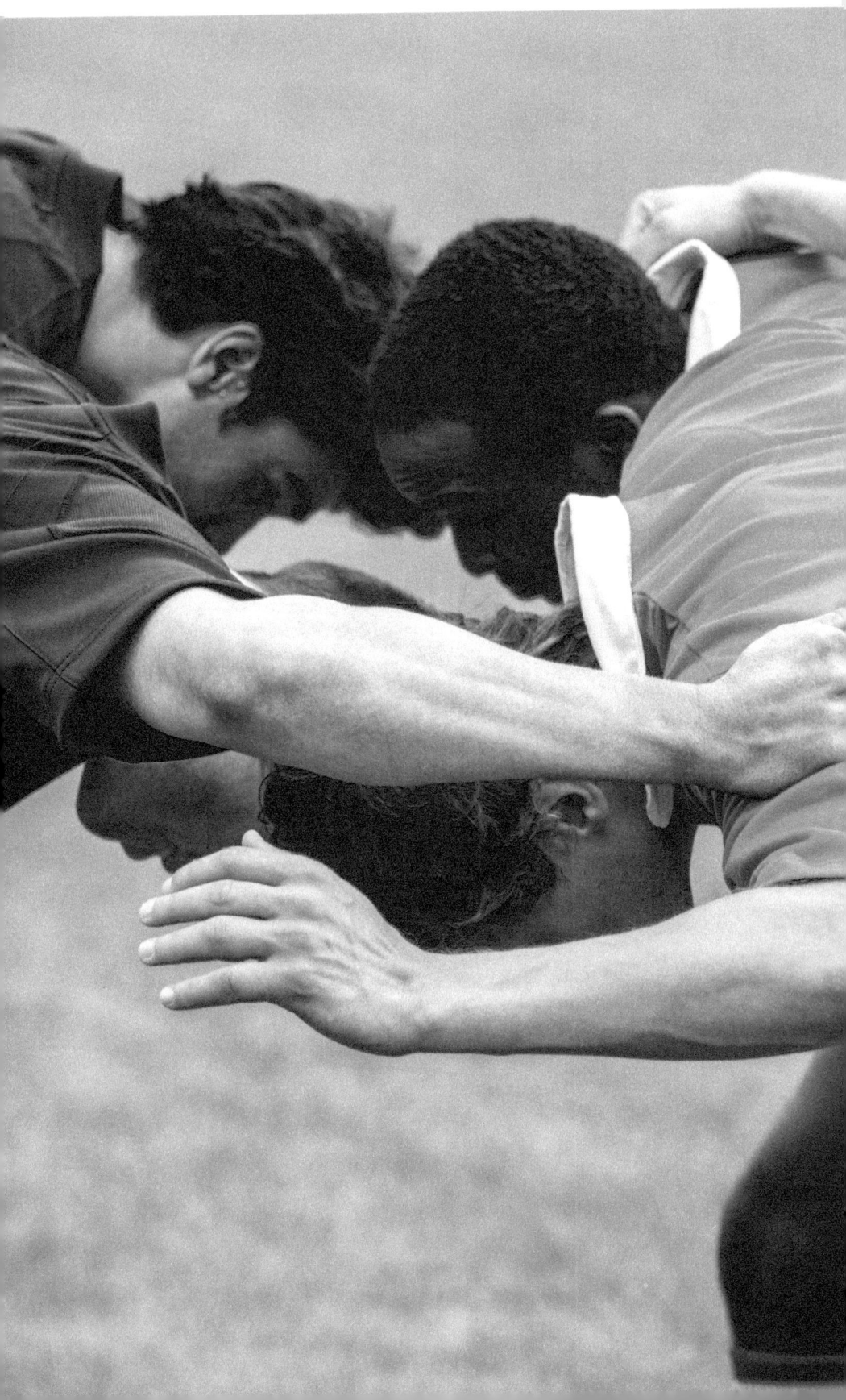

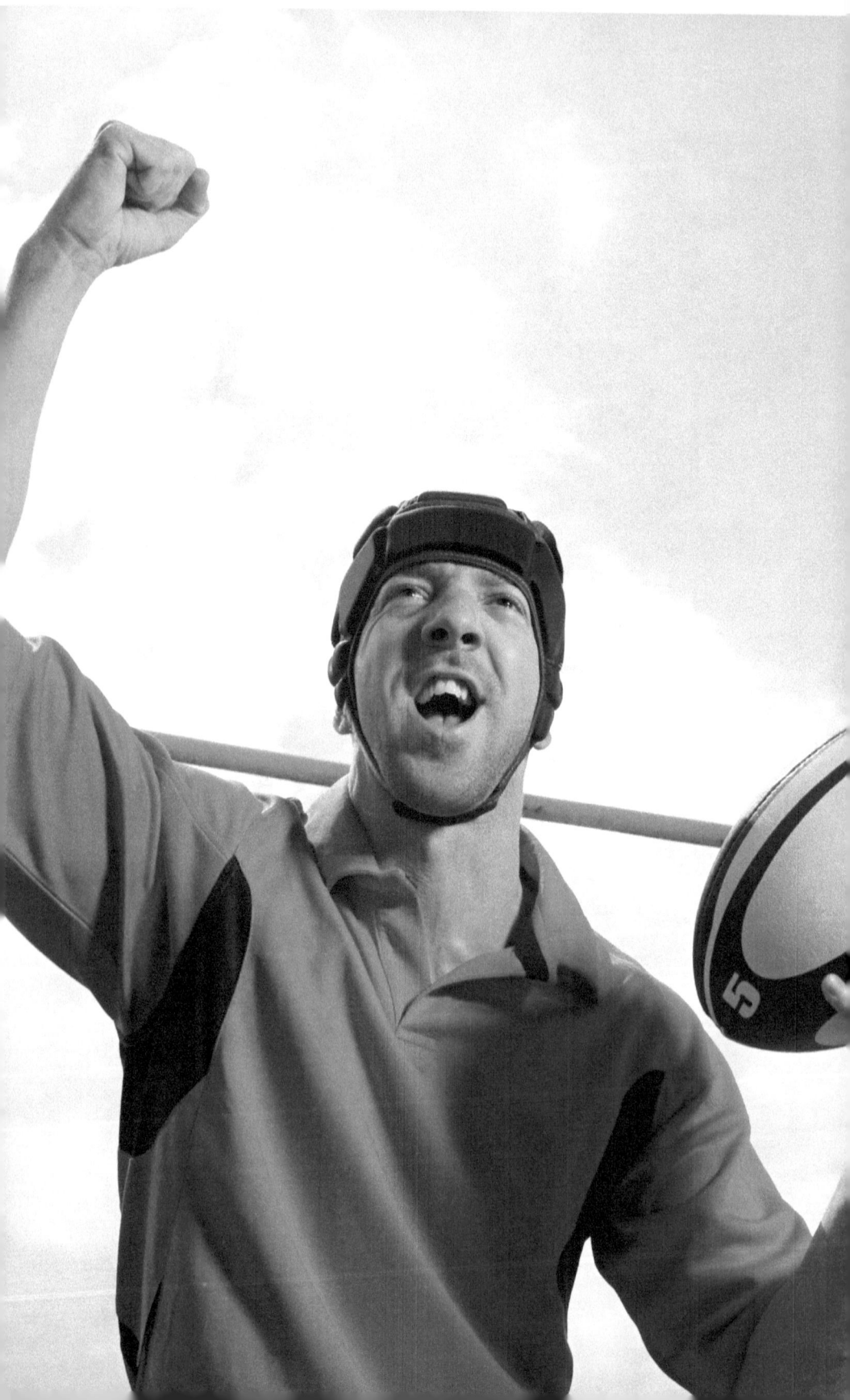

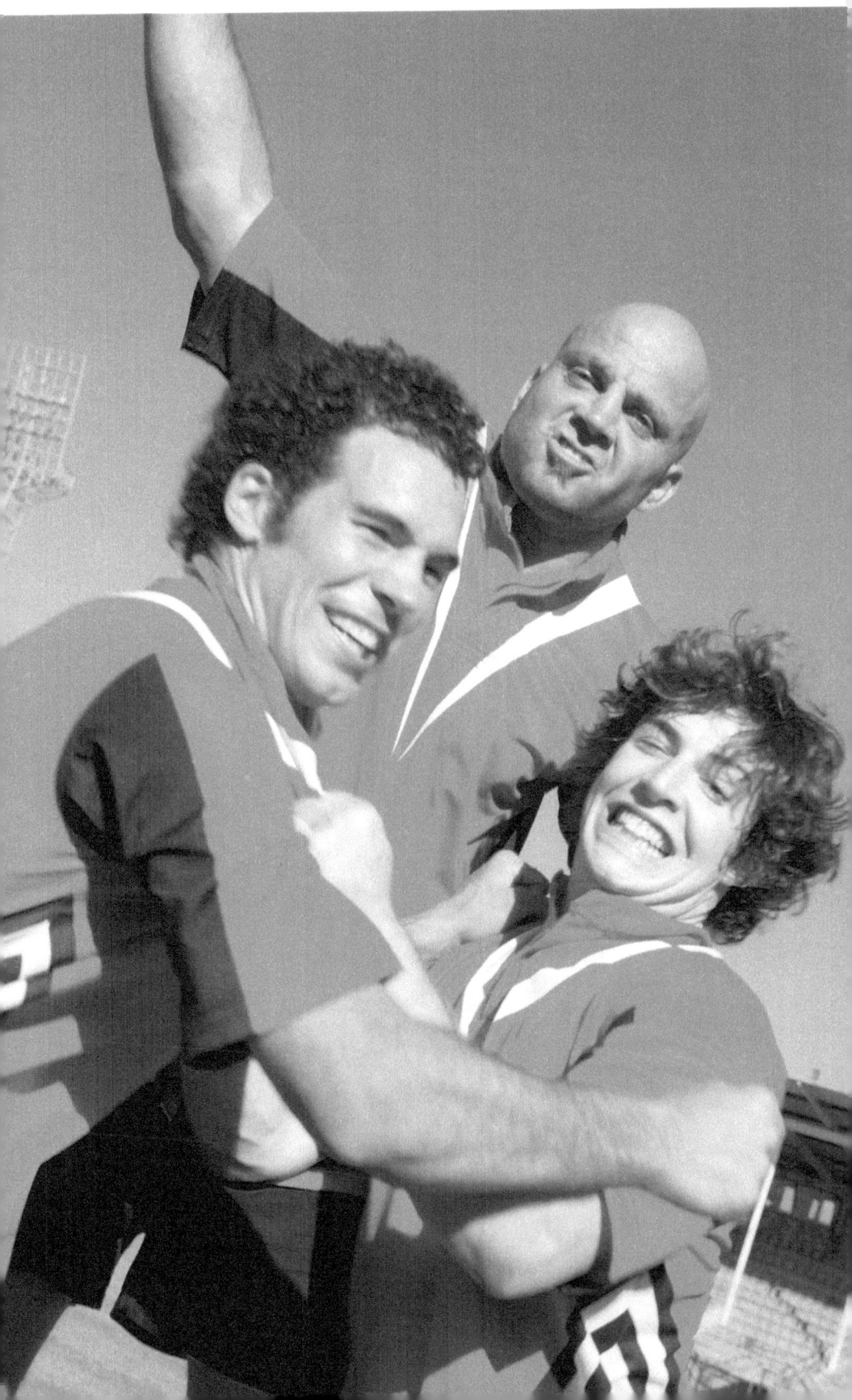

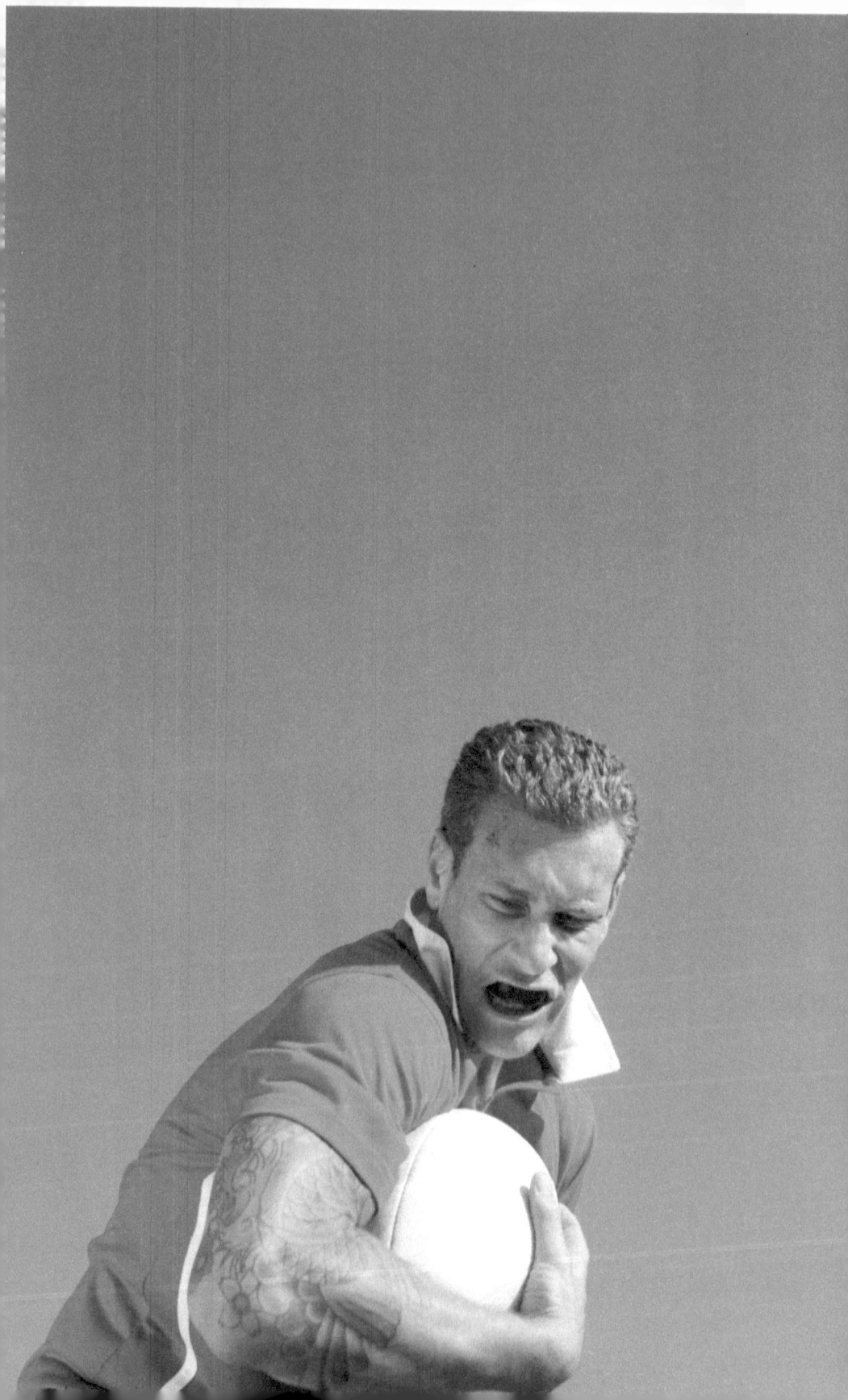

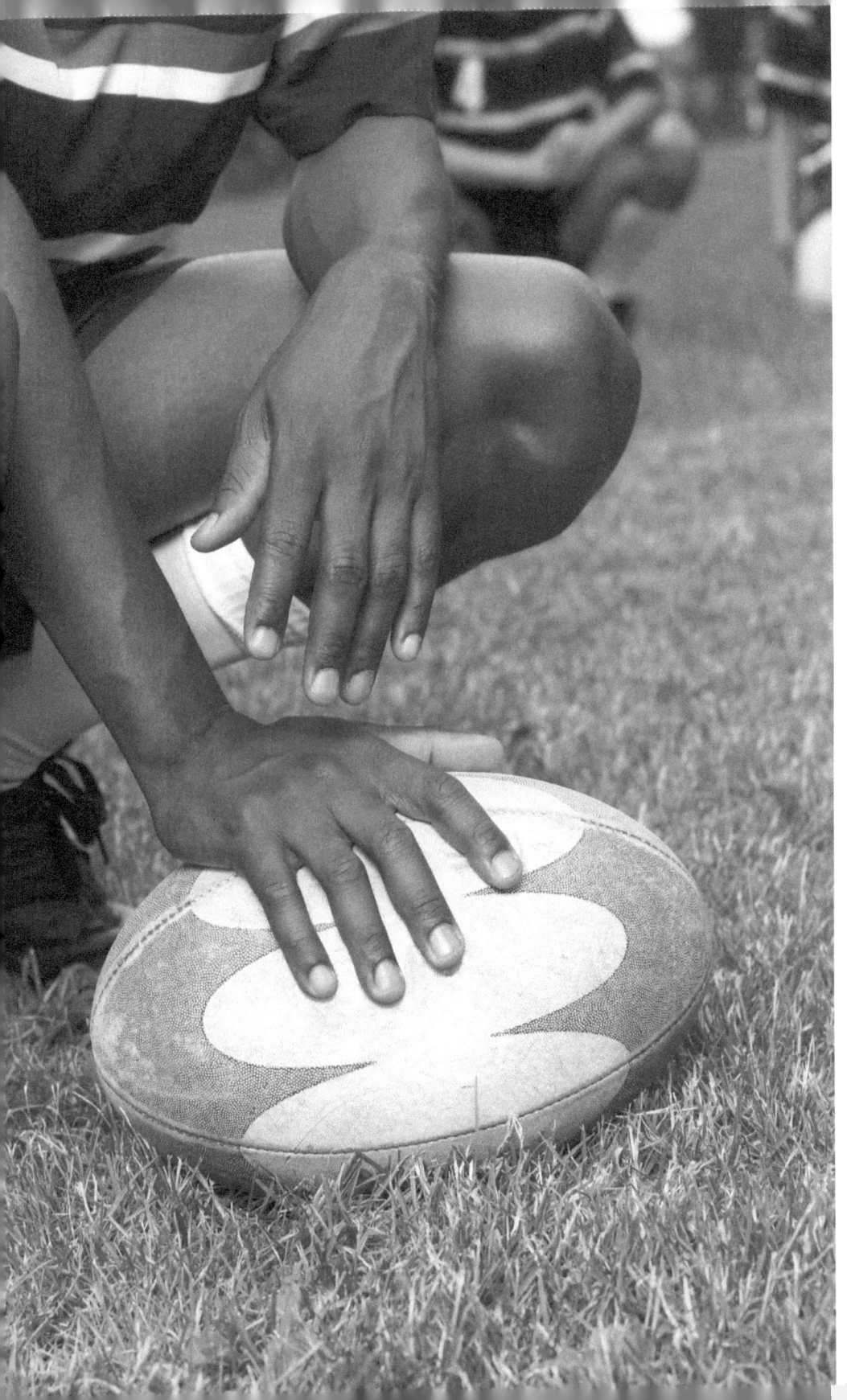

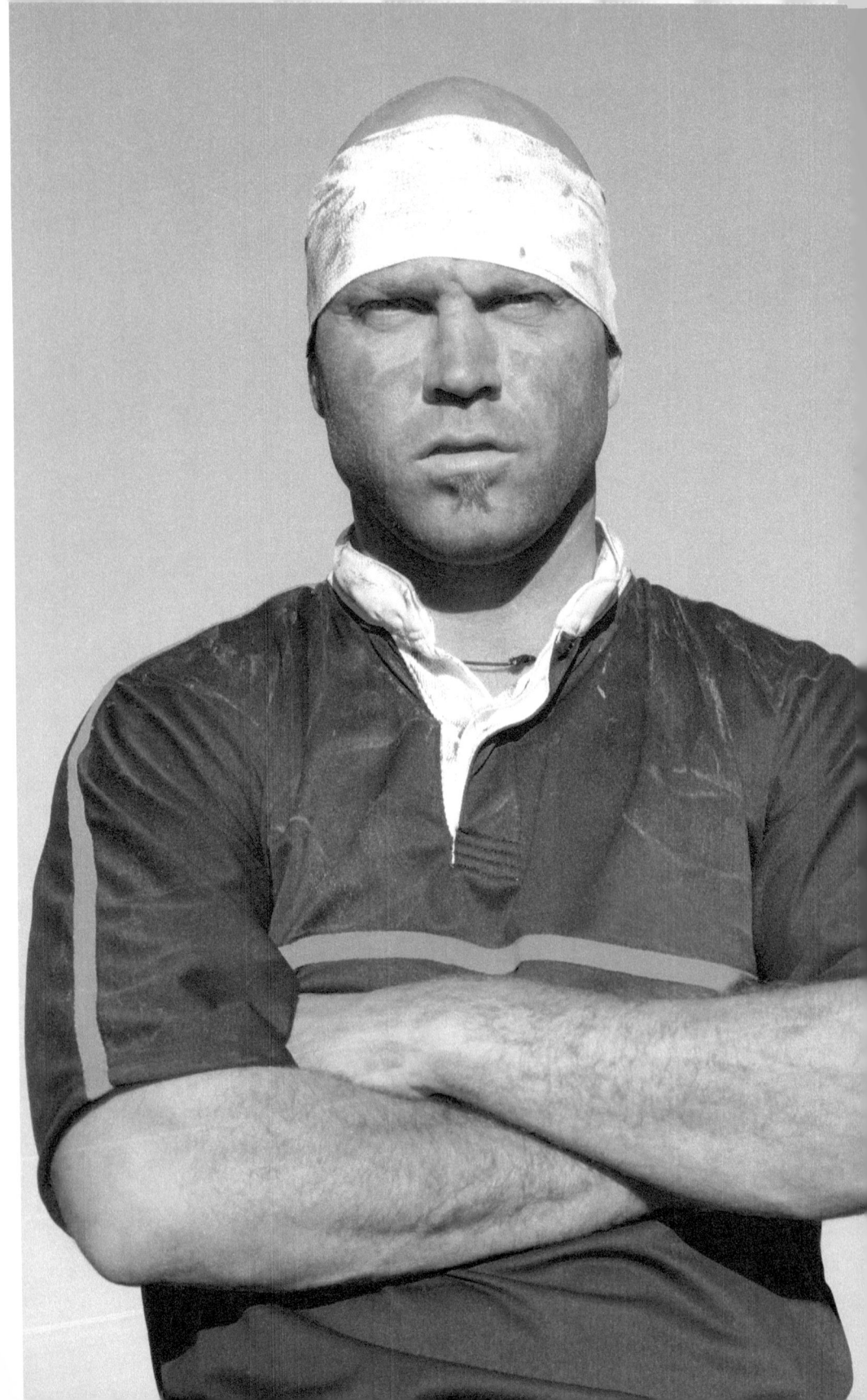

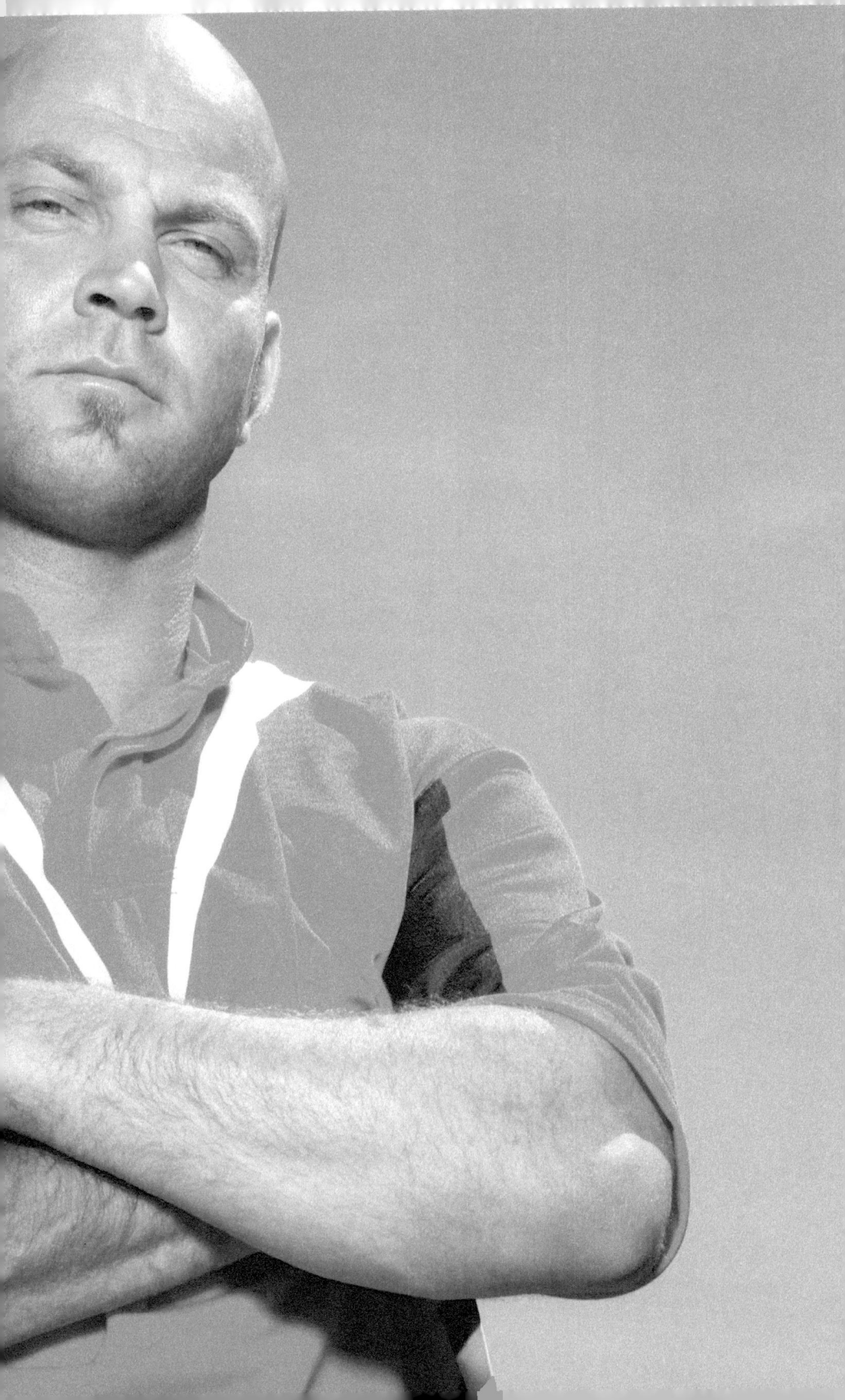

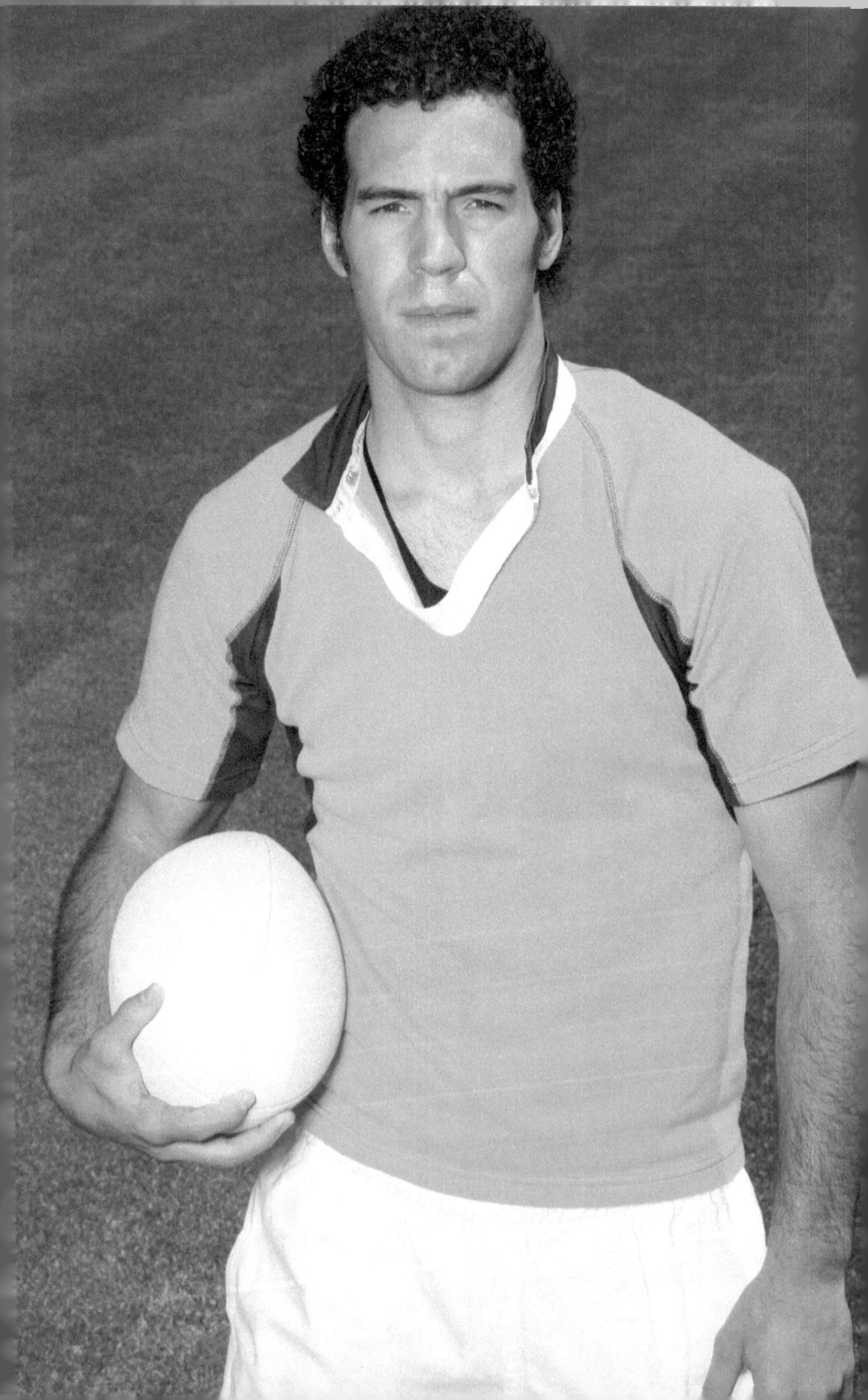

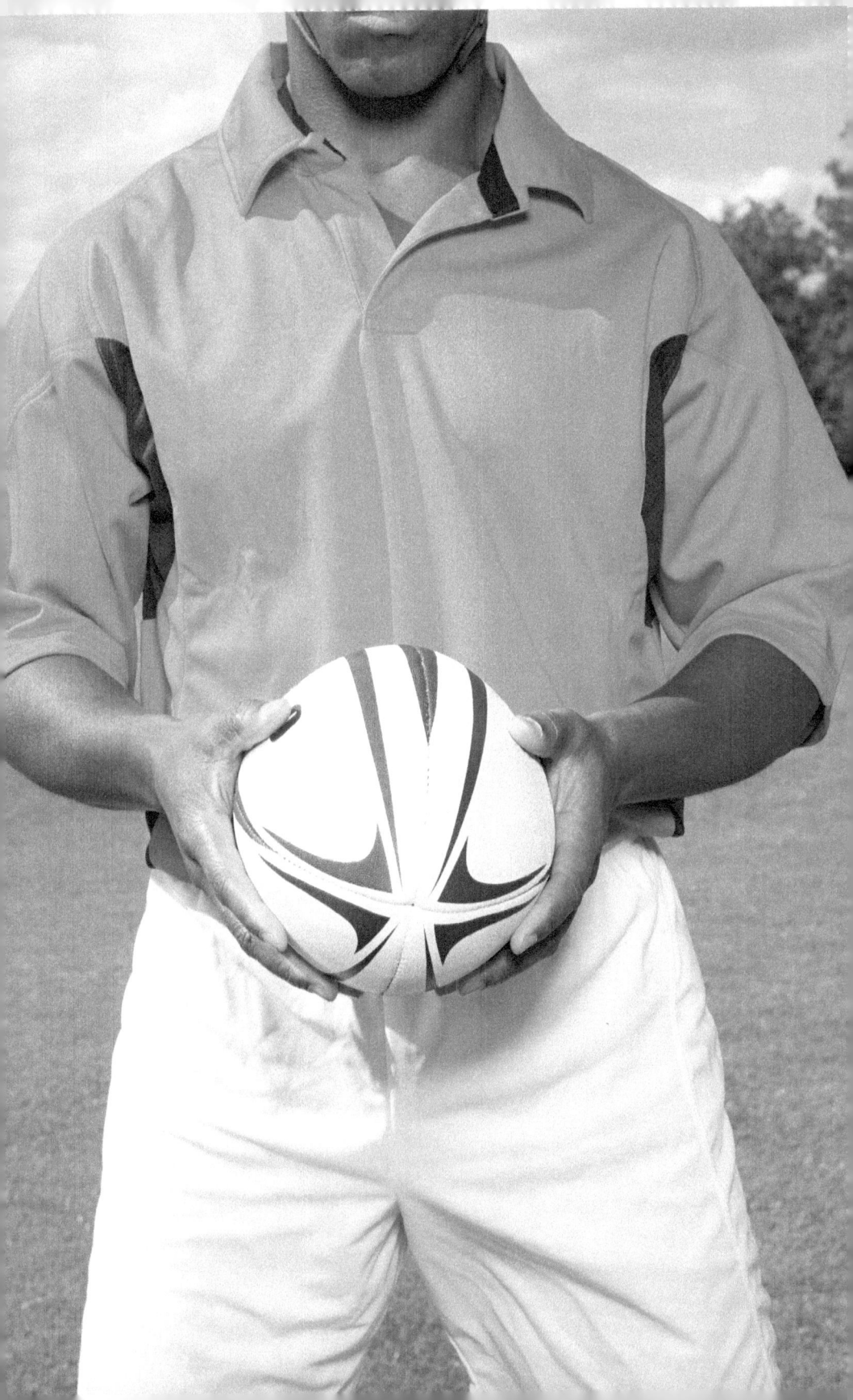

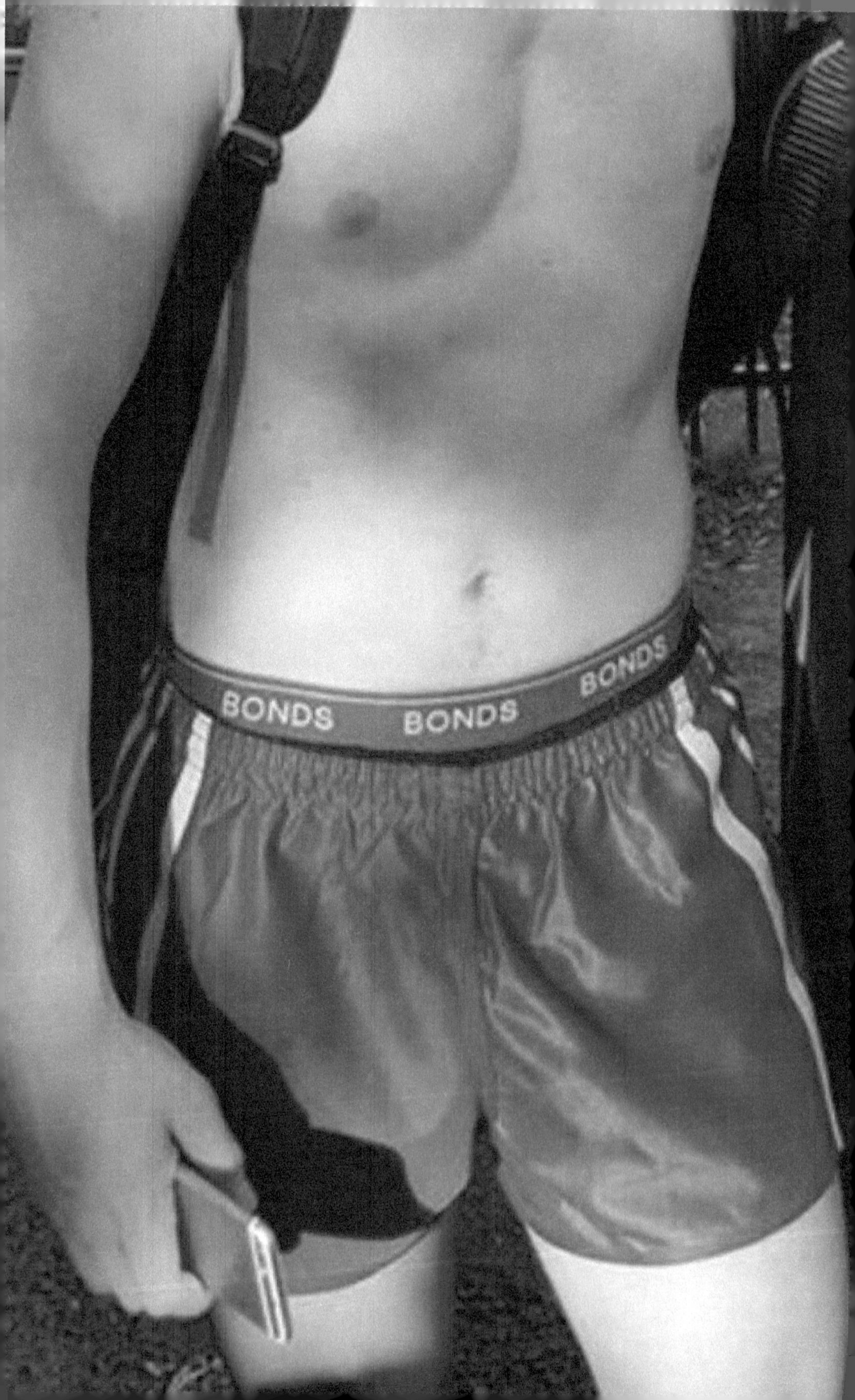
BONDS
BONDS
BONDS

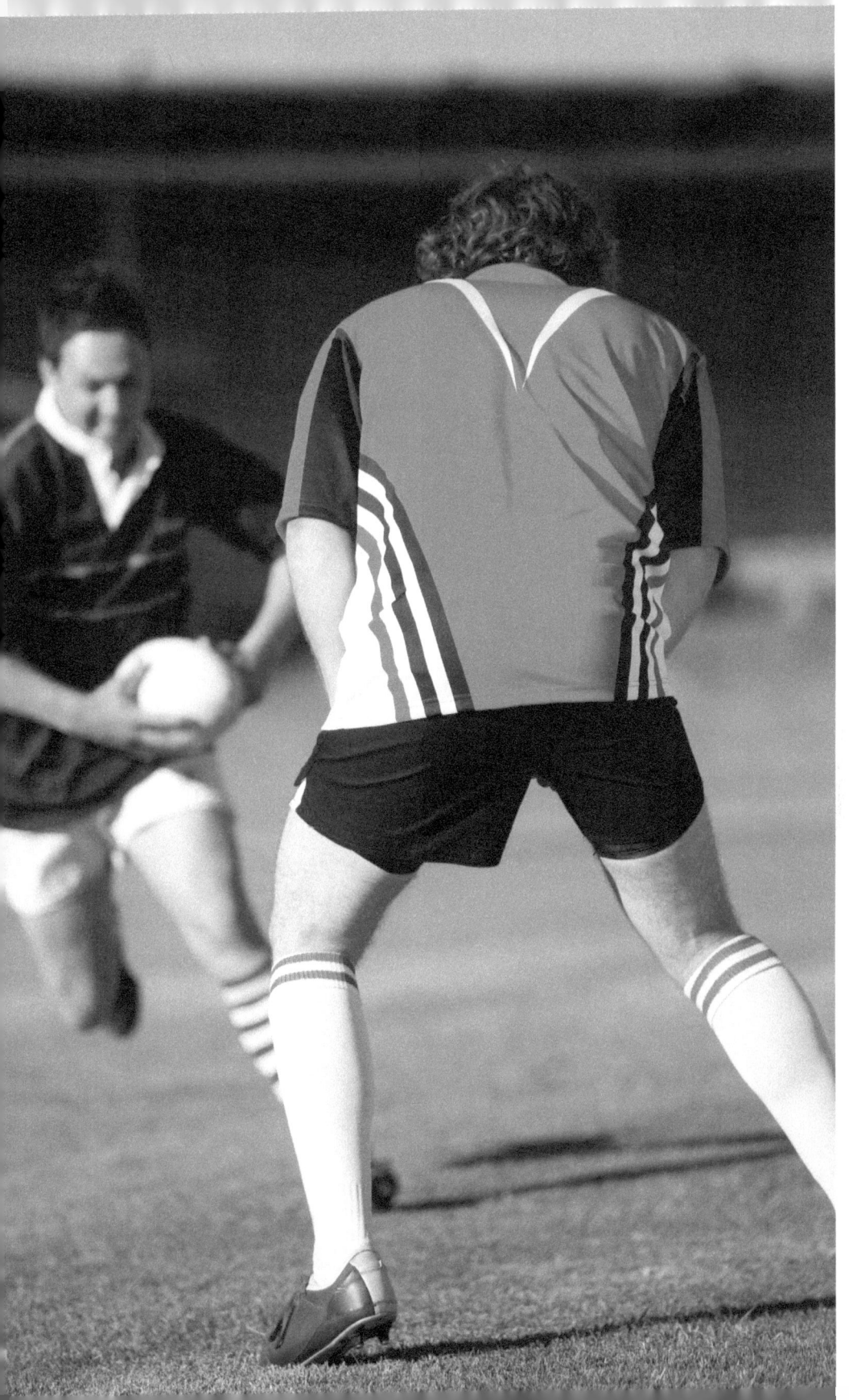

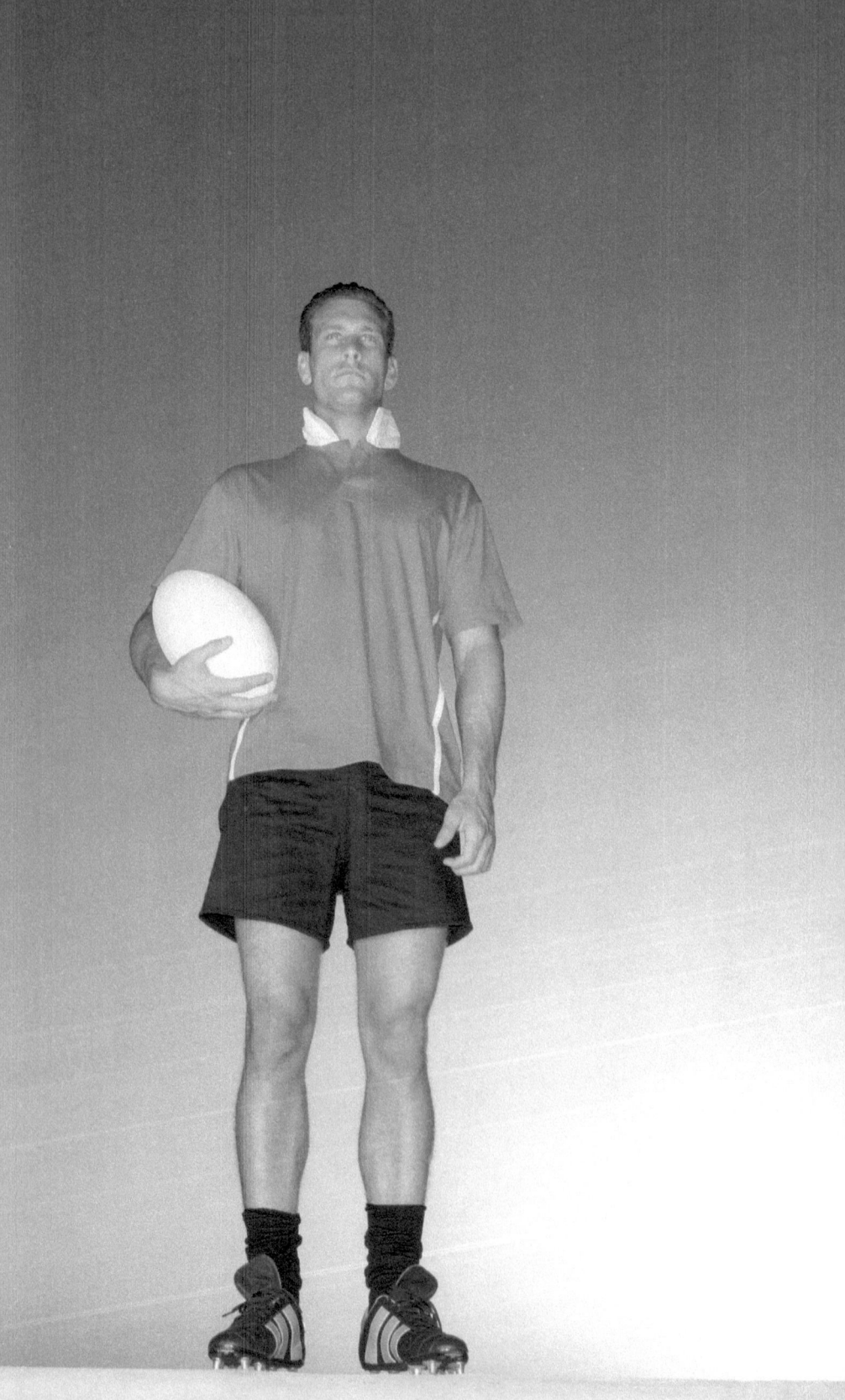

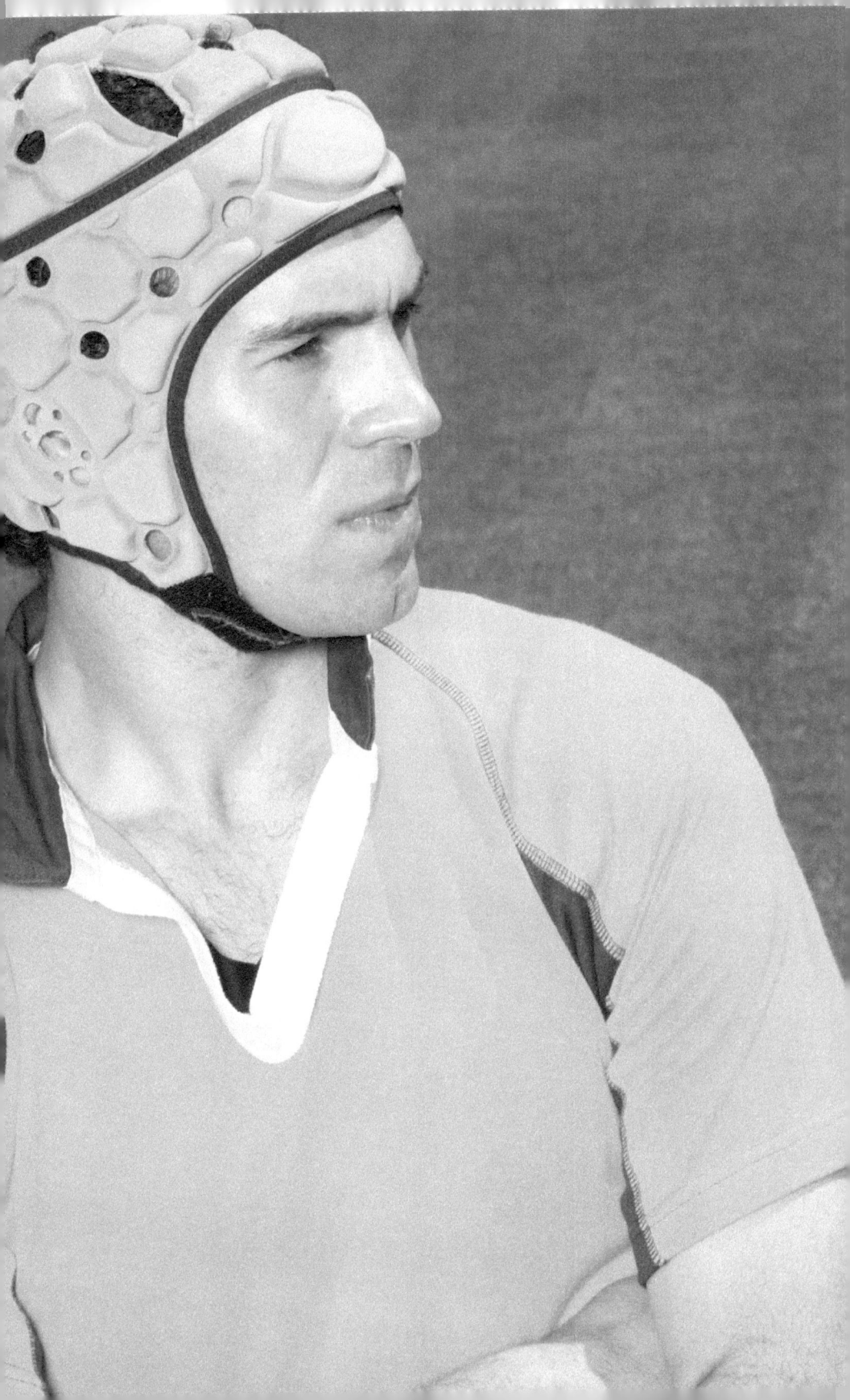

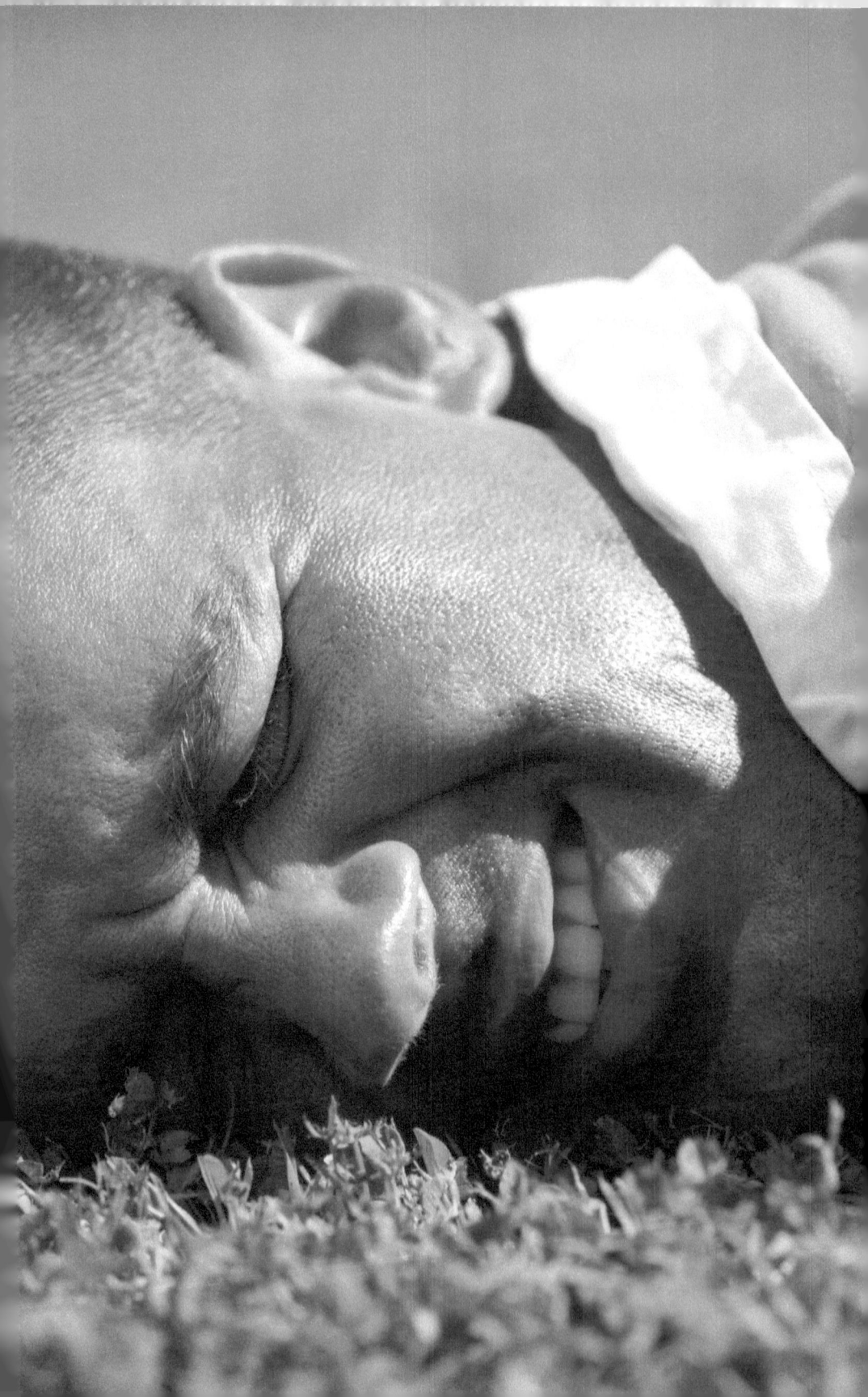

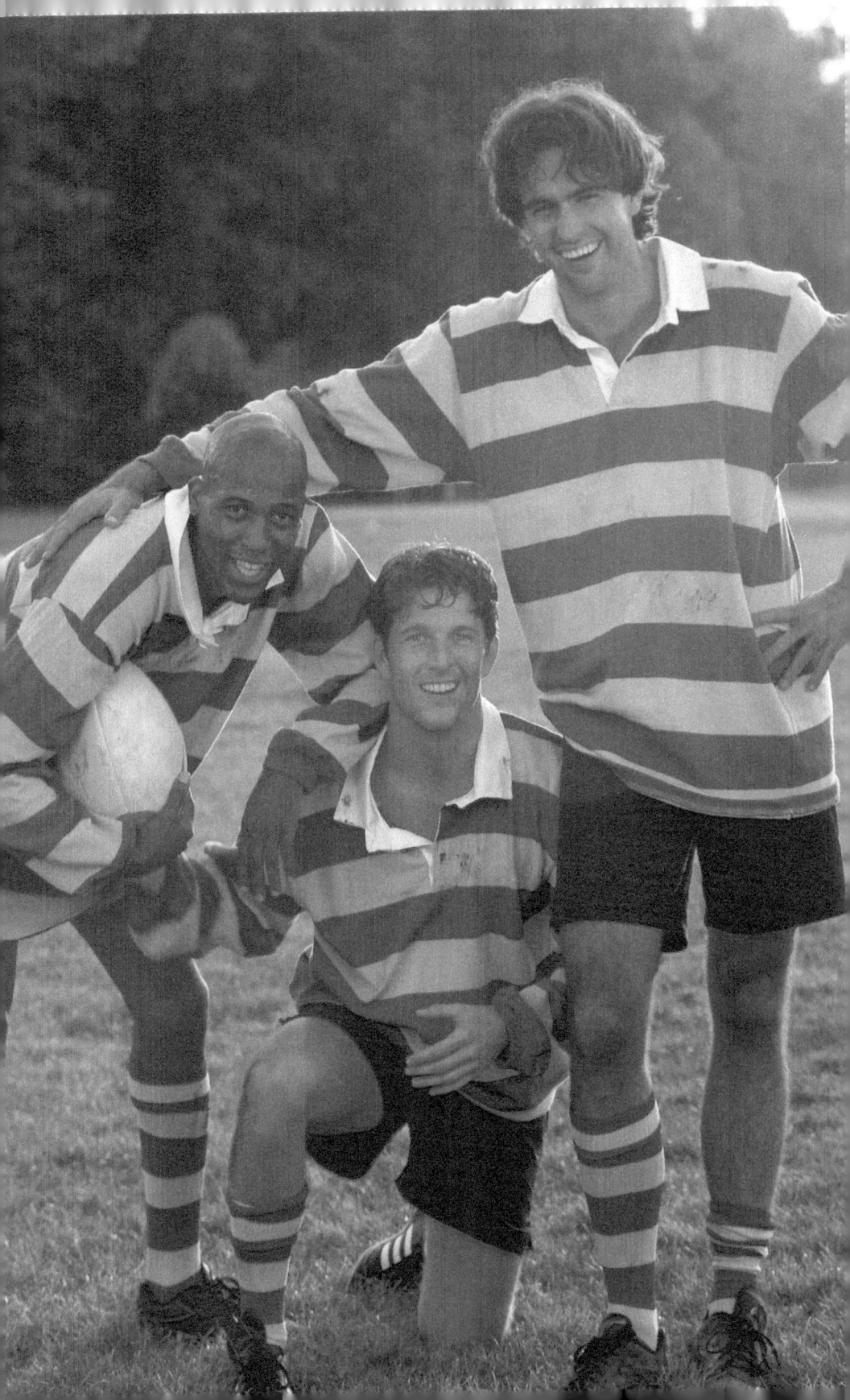

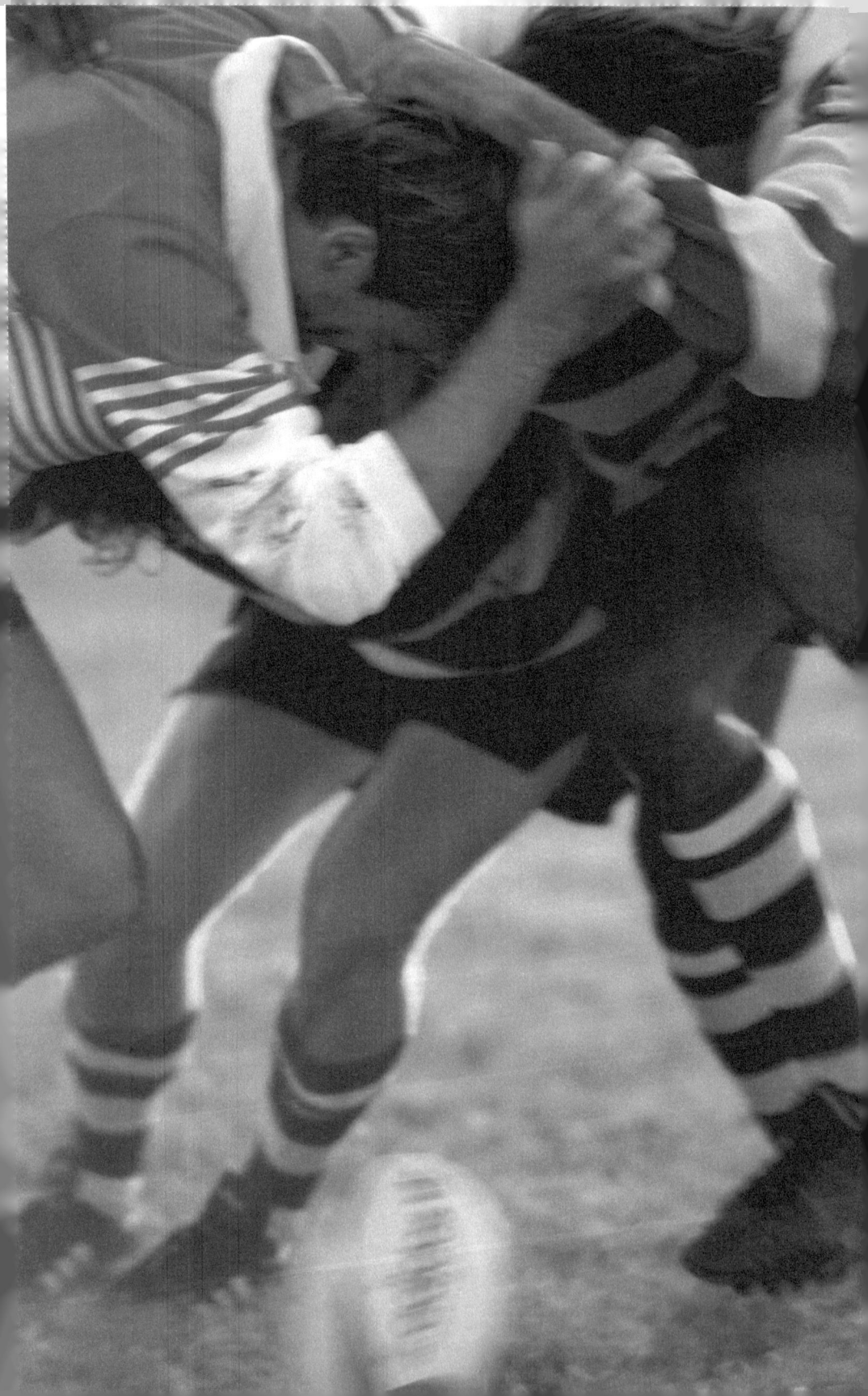

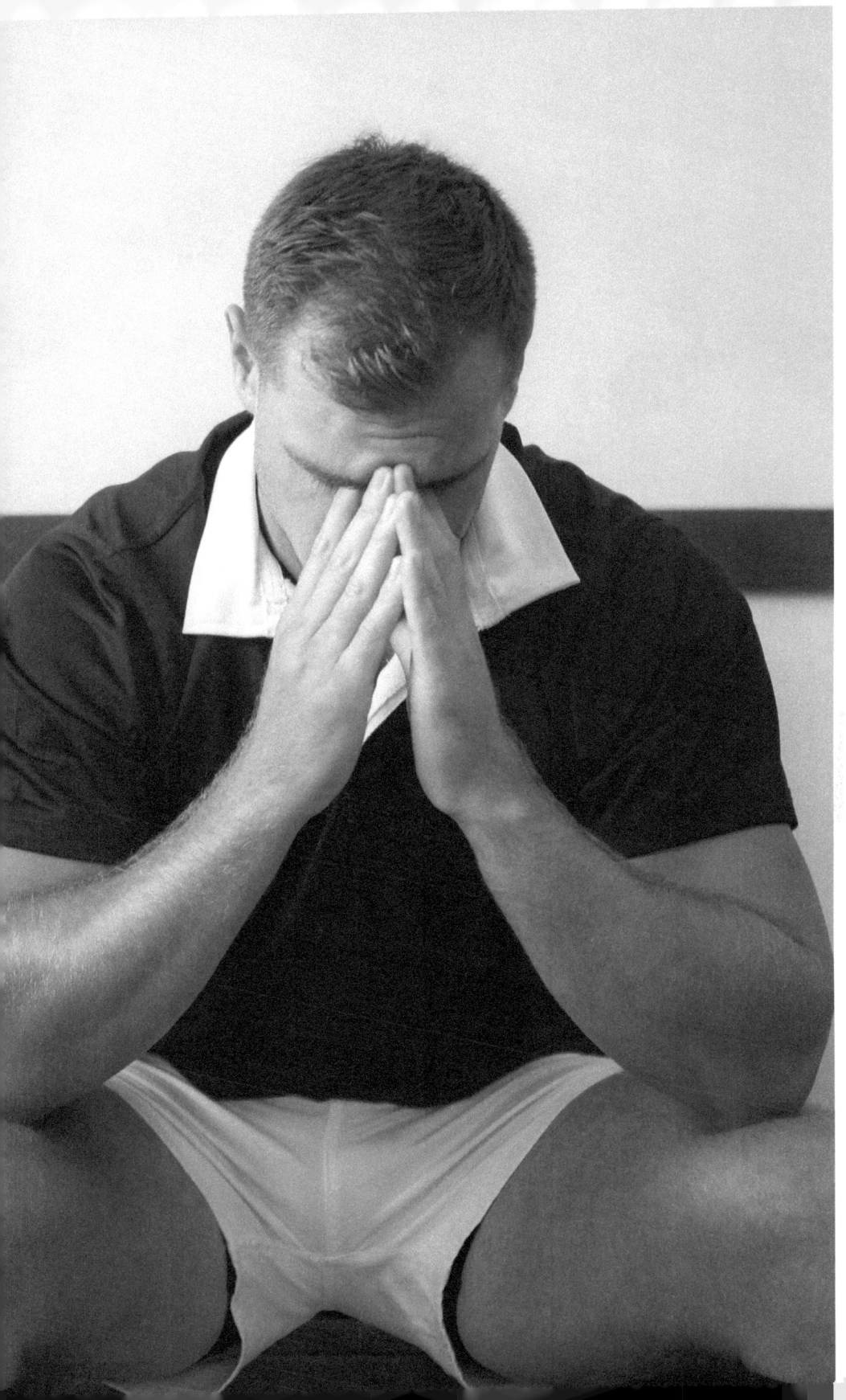

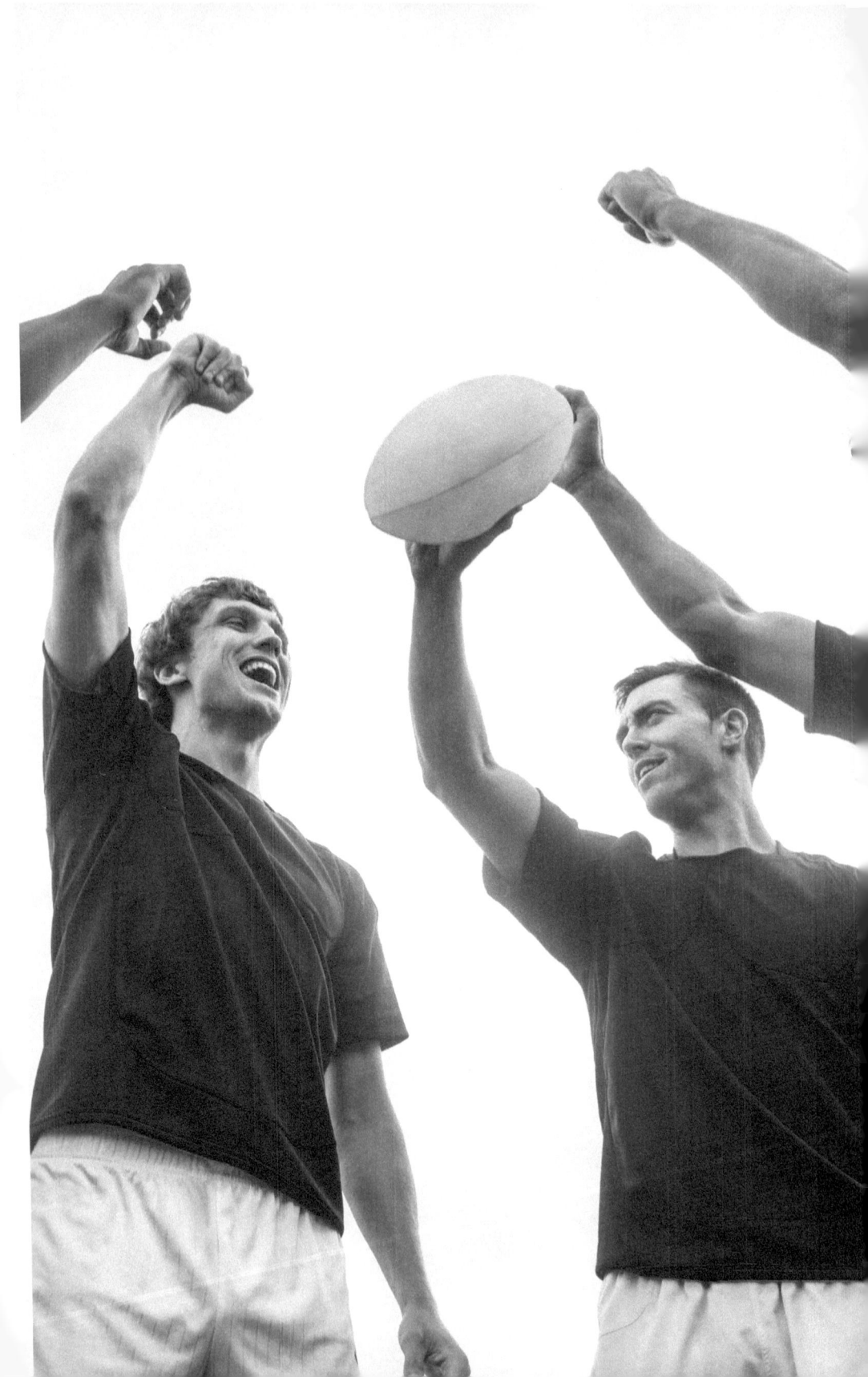

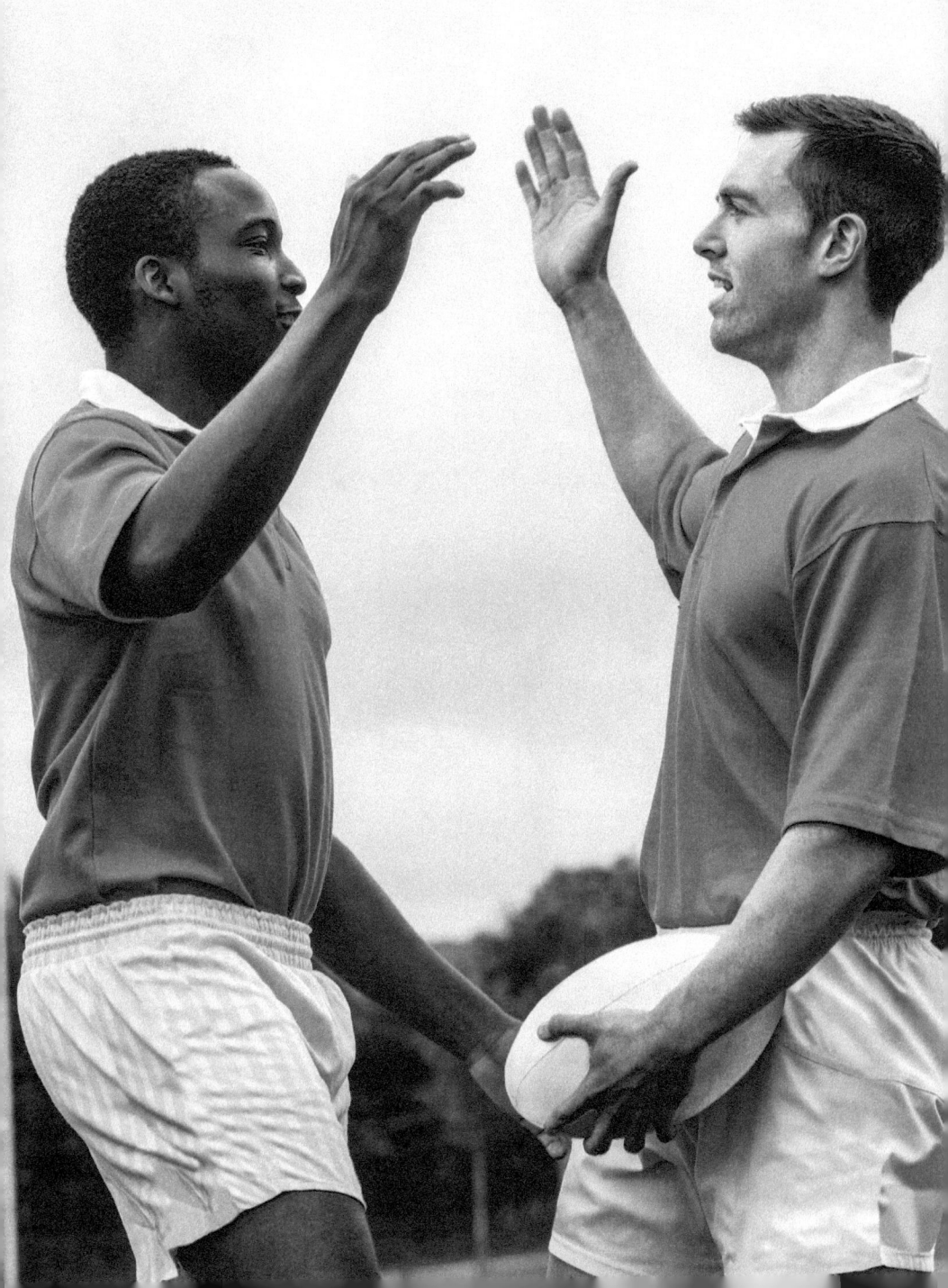

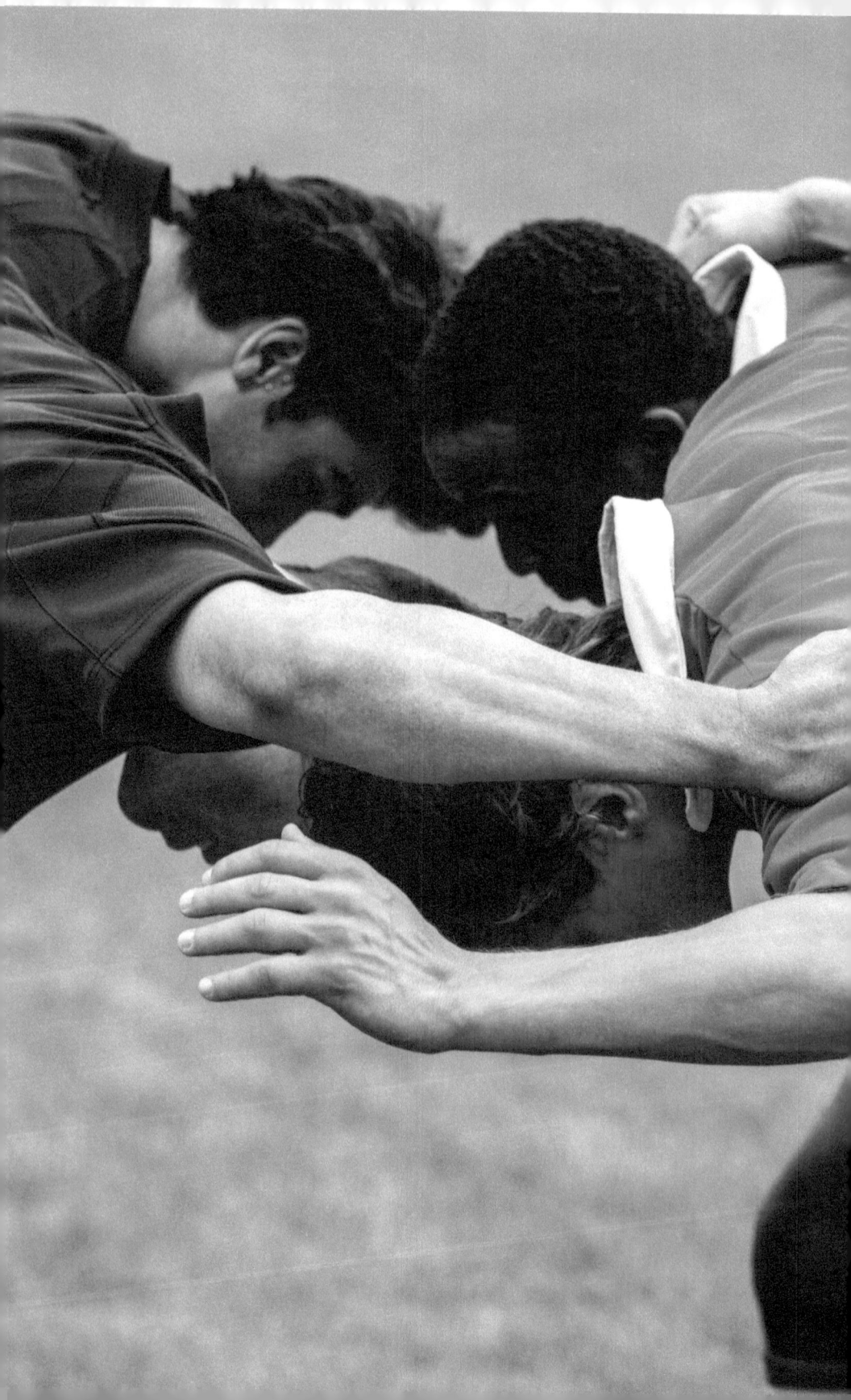

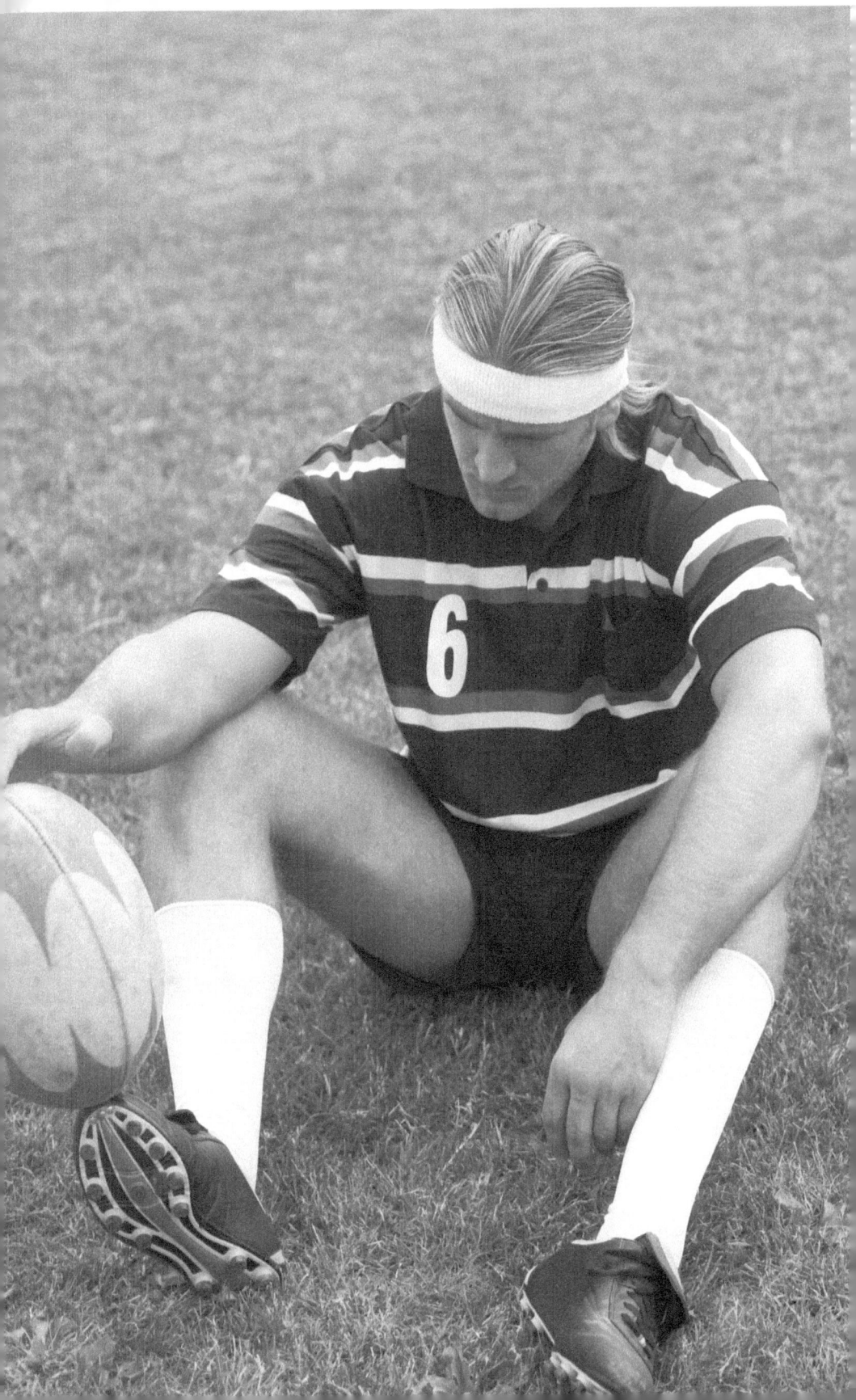

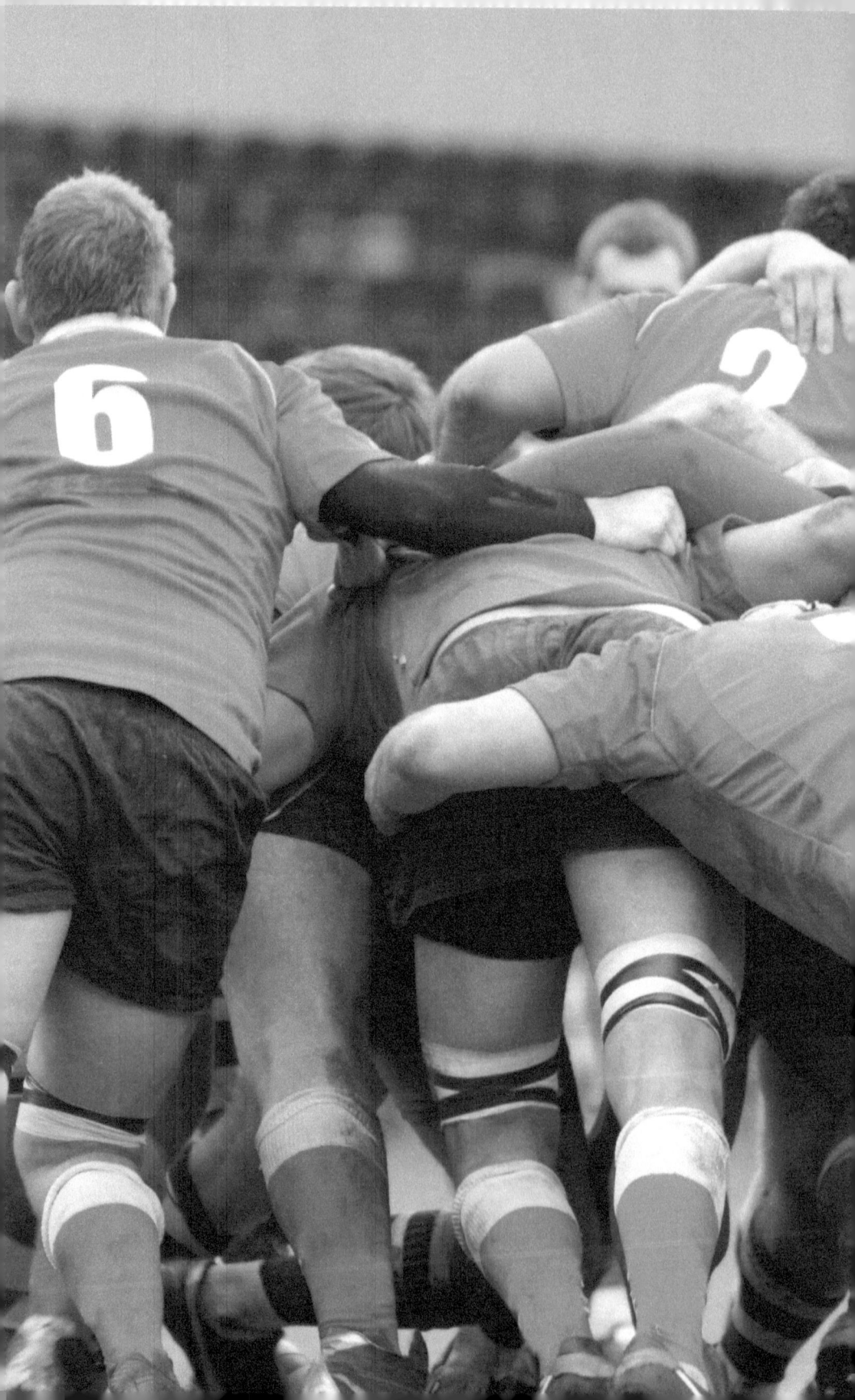

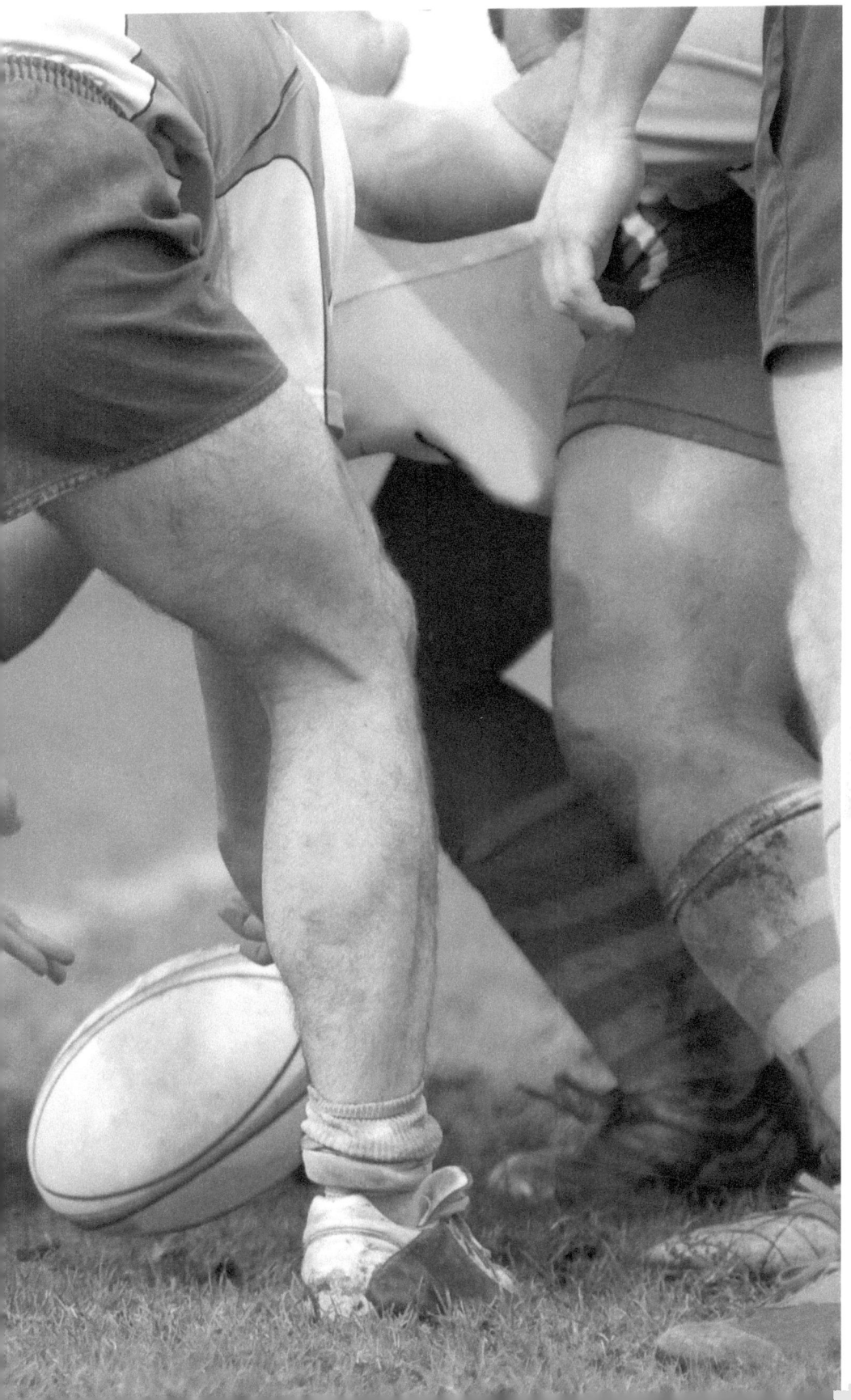

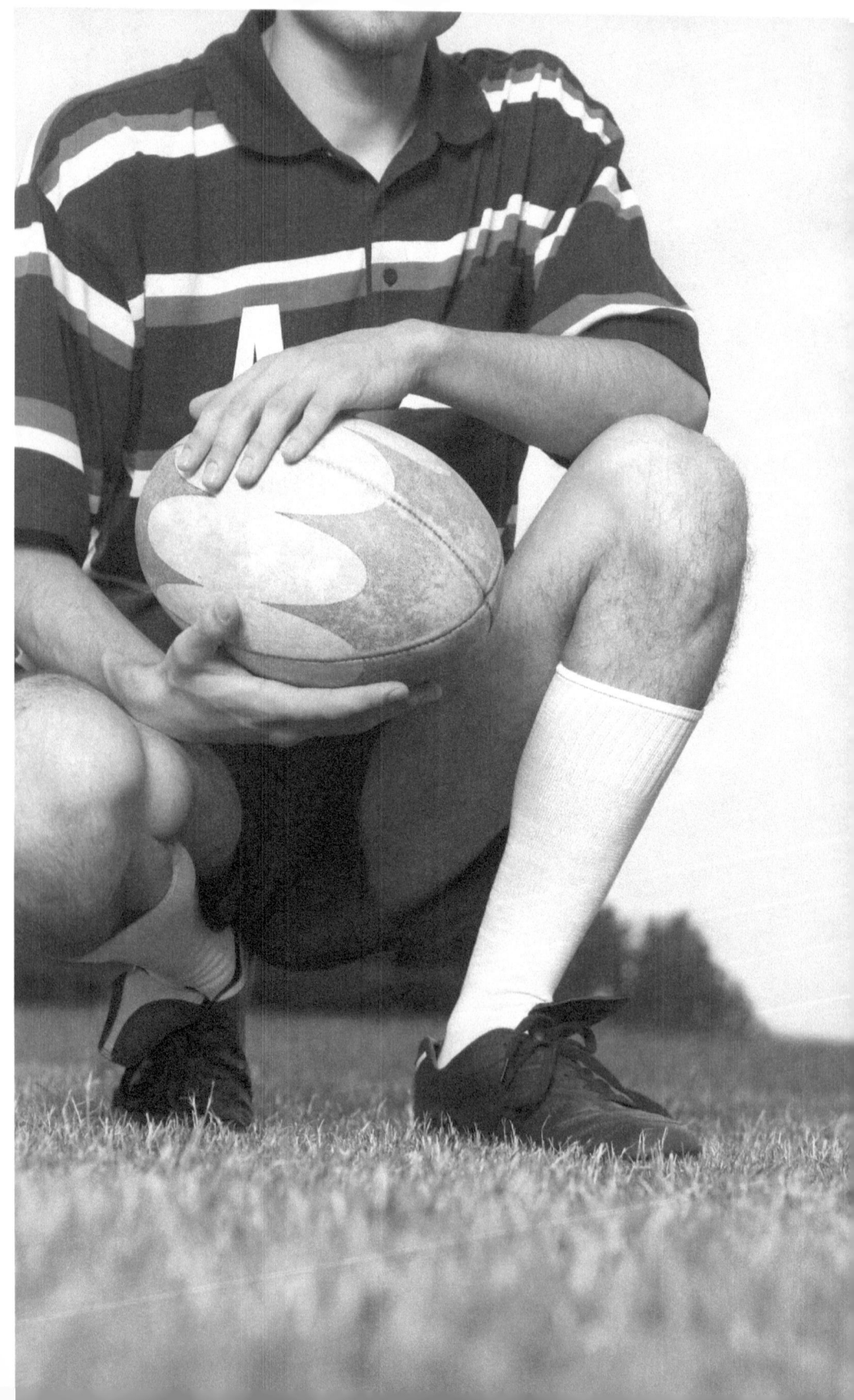

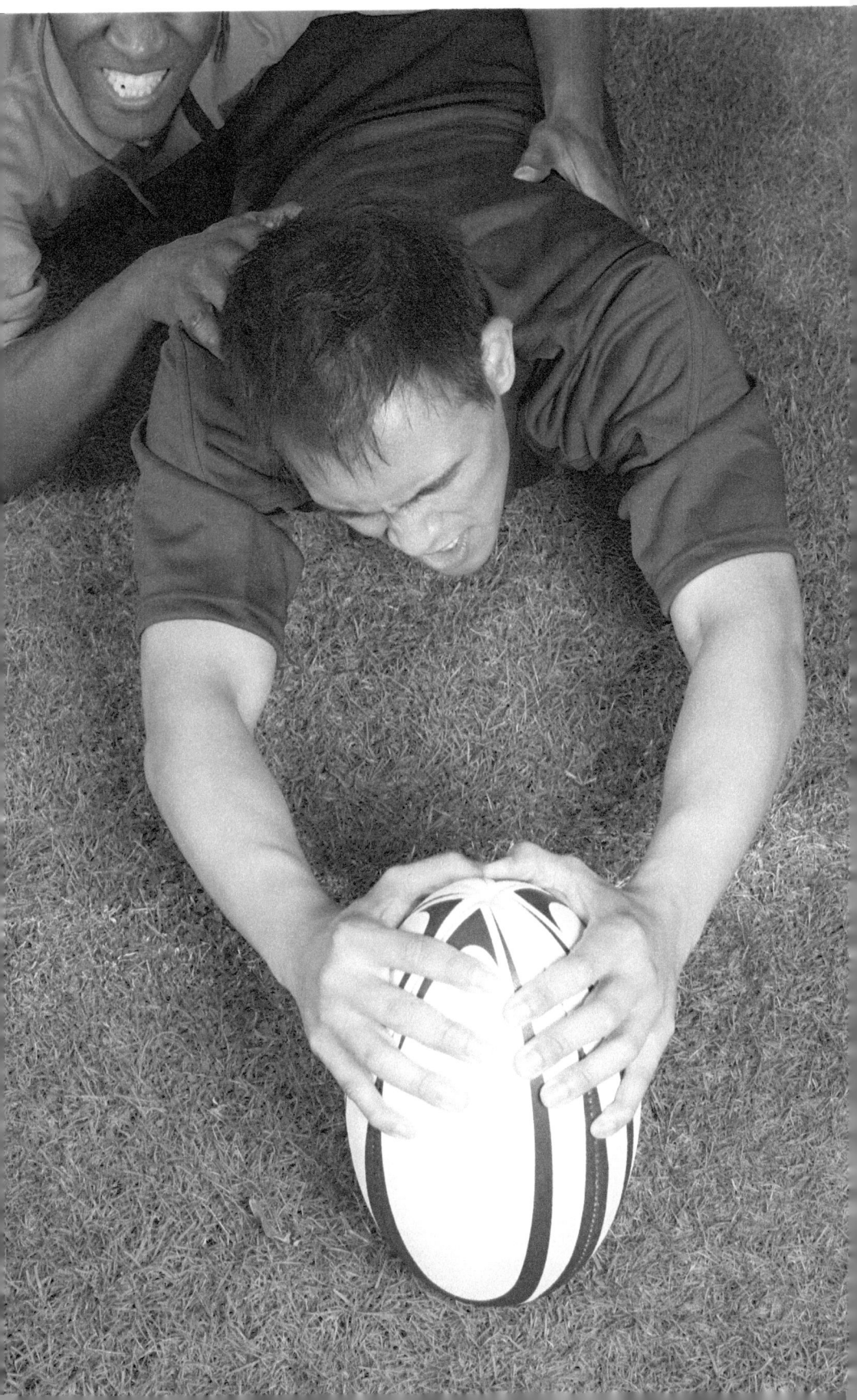

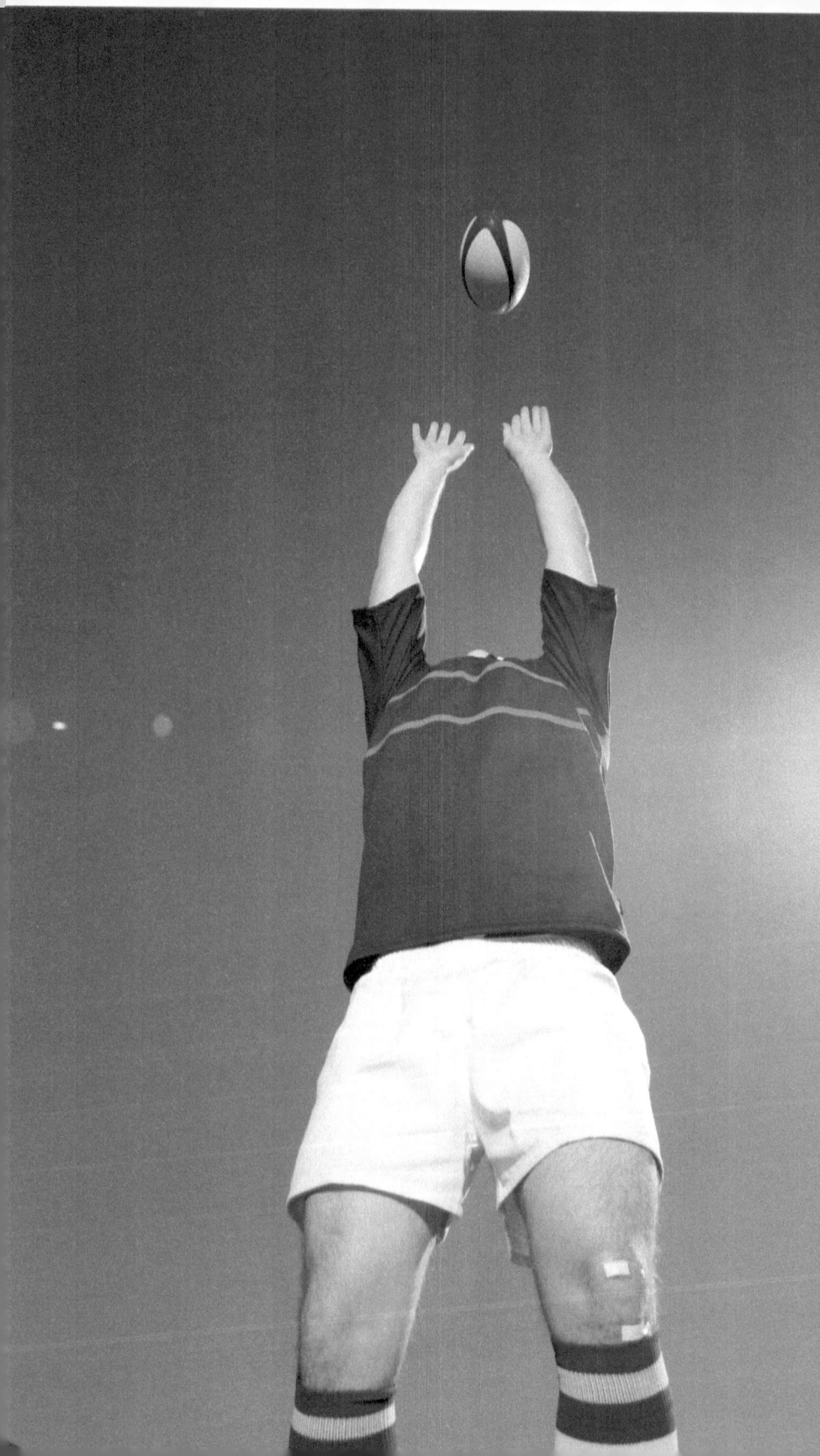

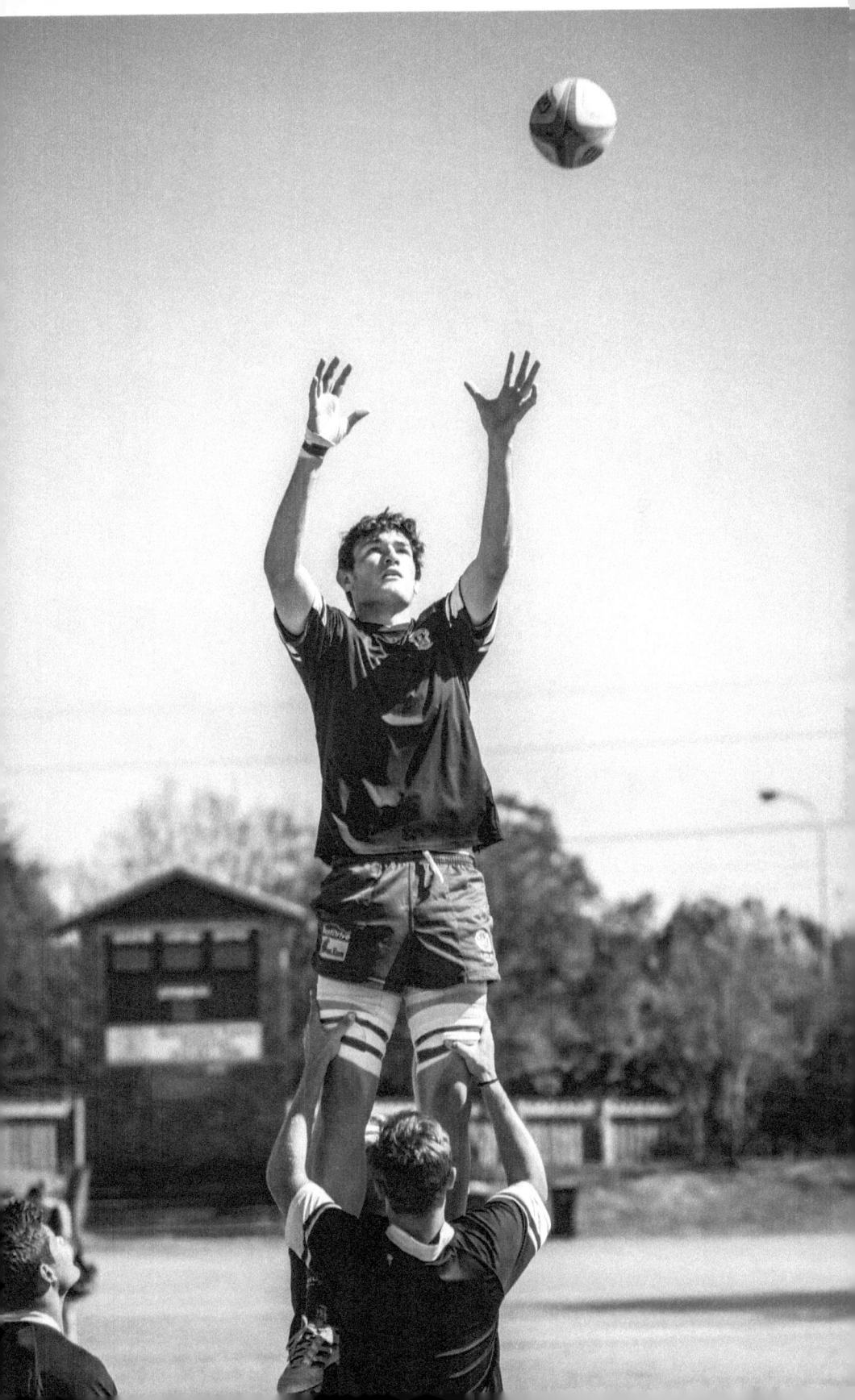

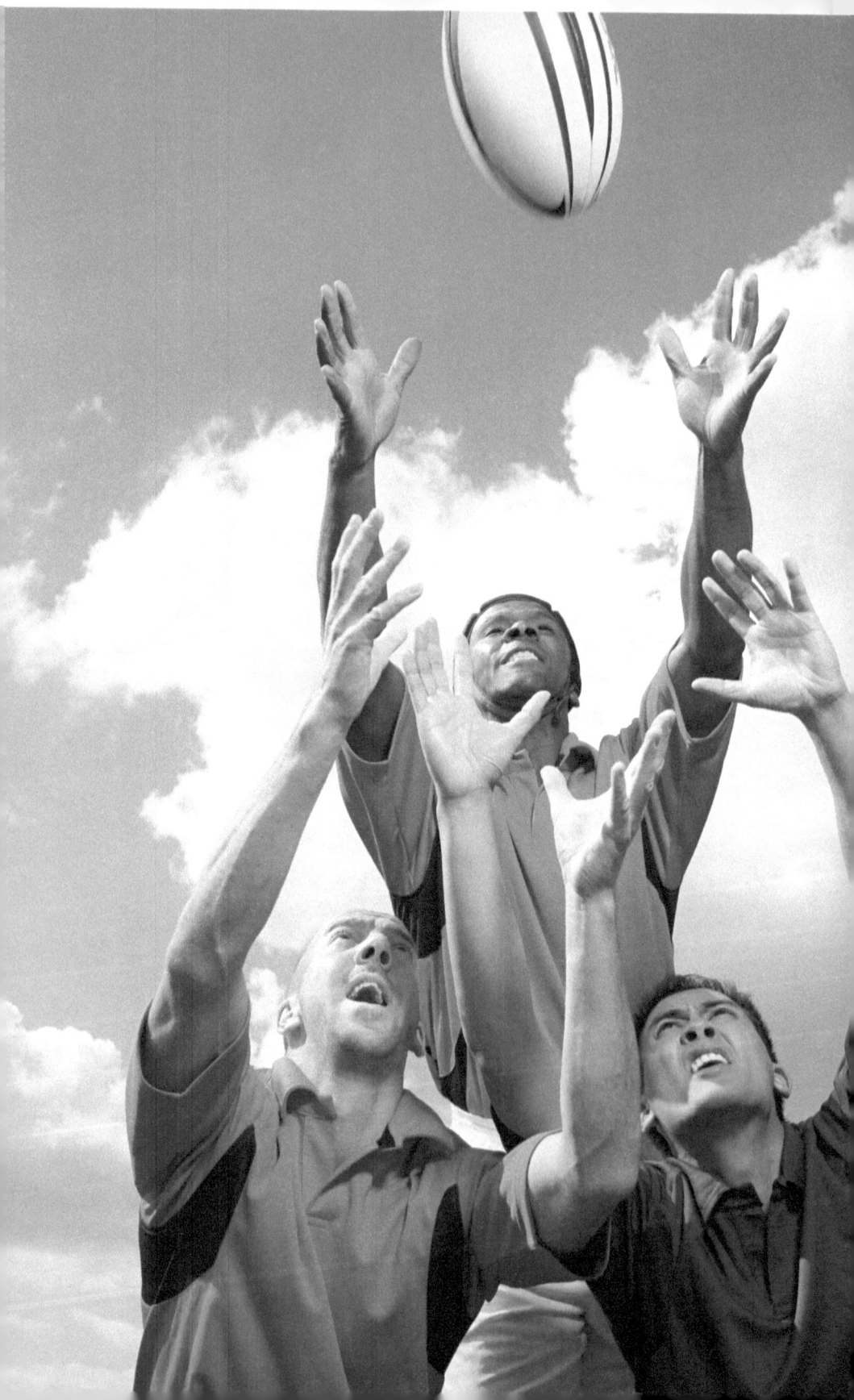

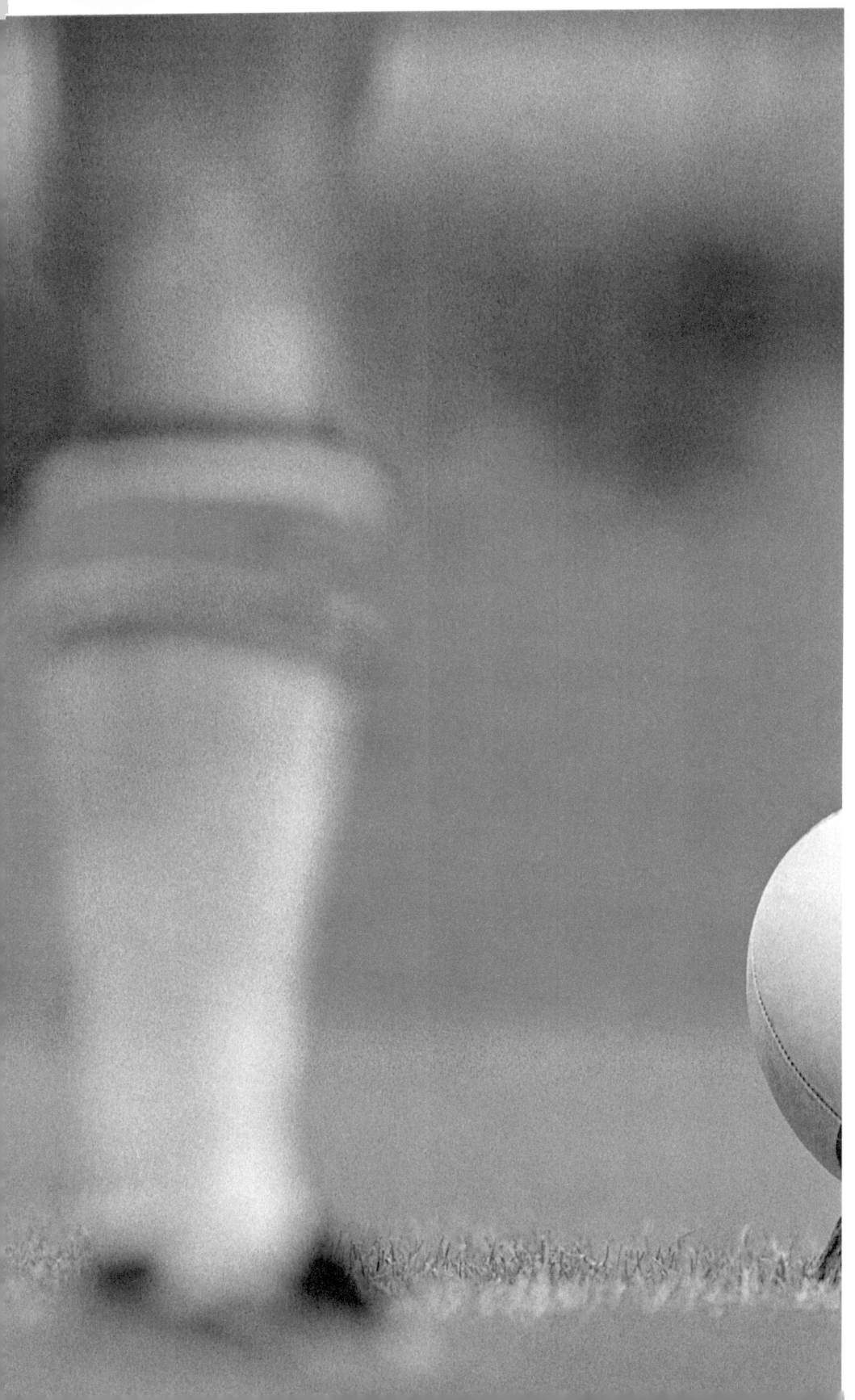

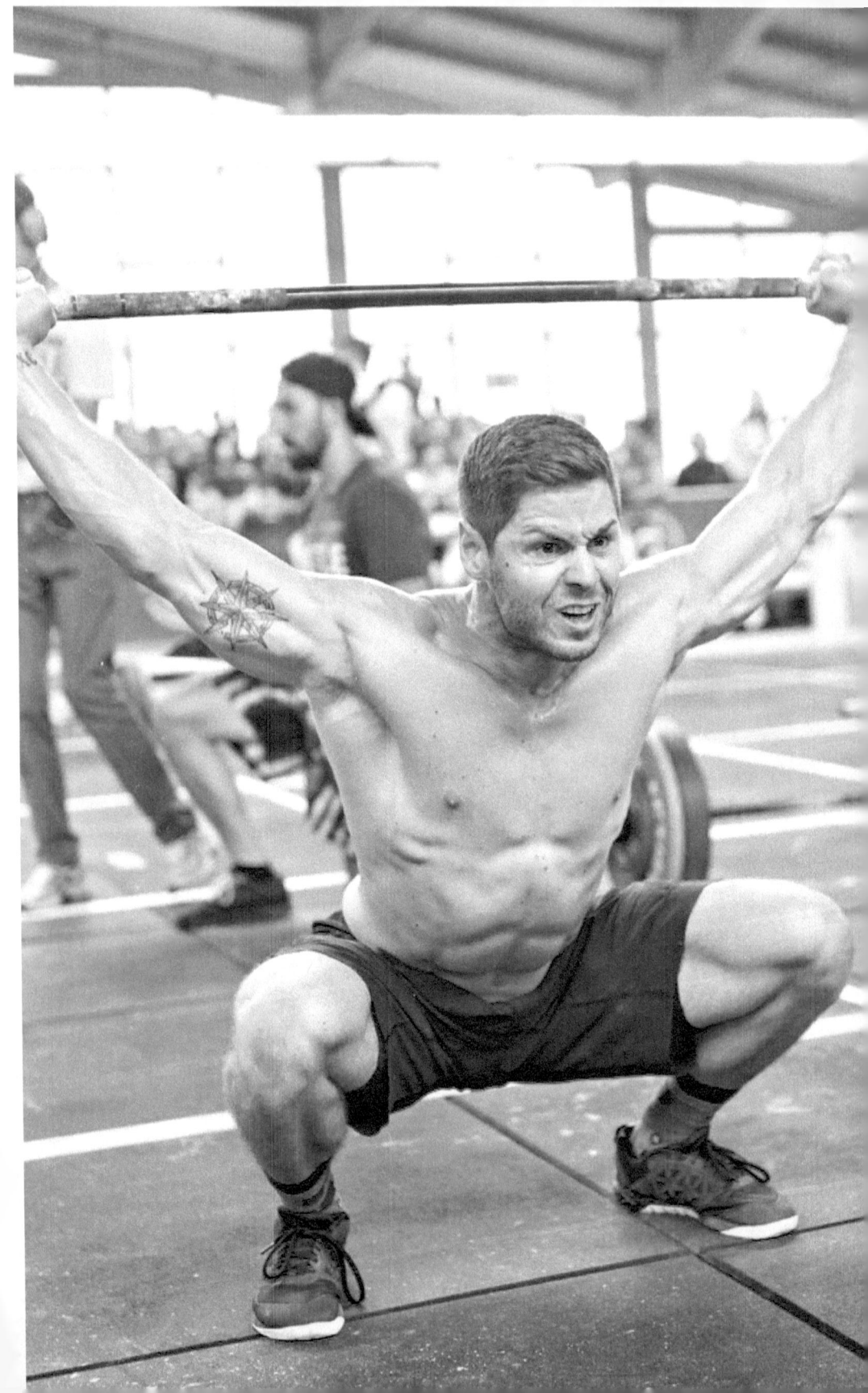

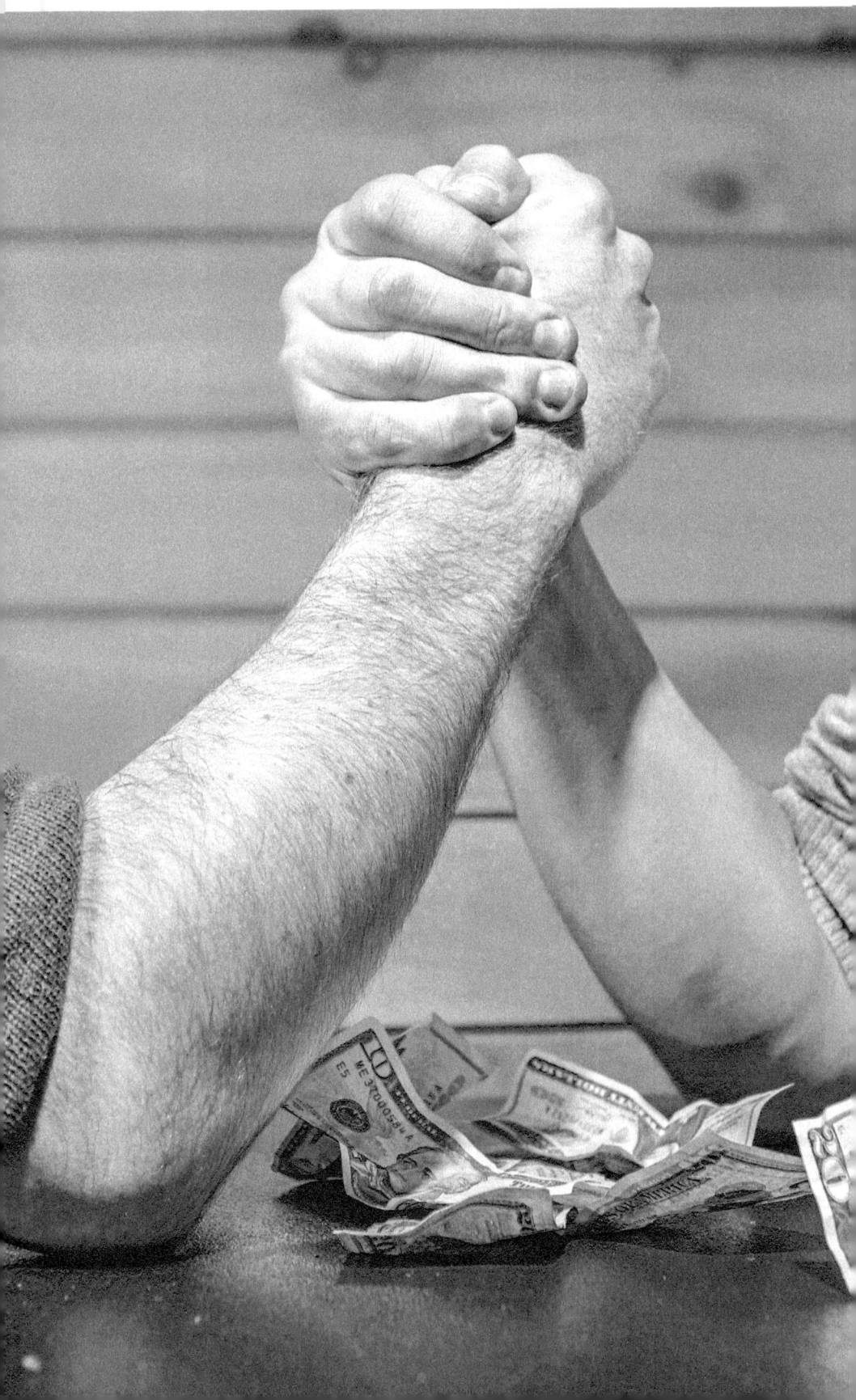

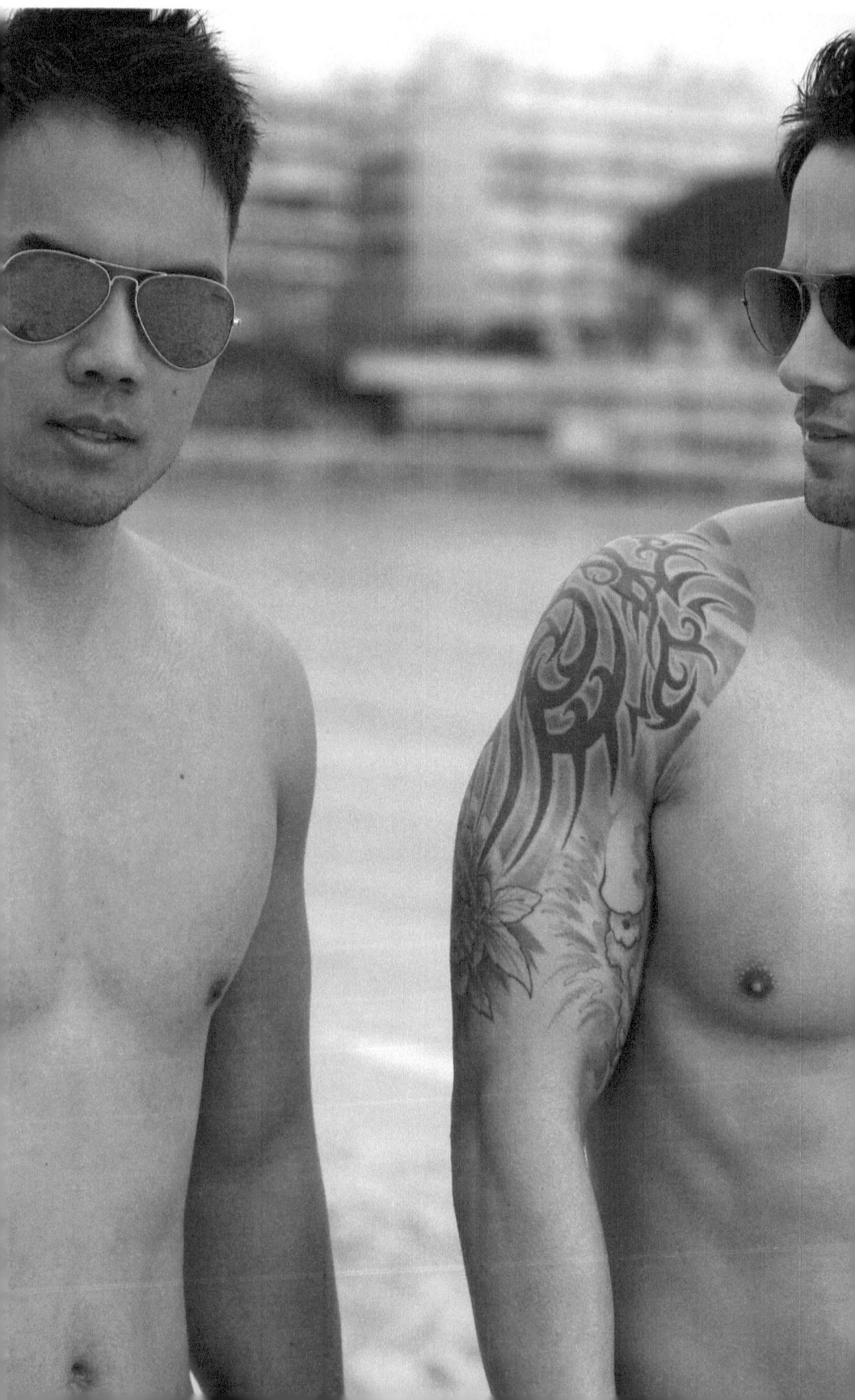

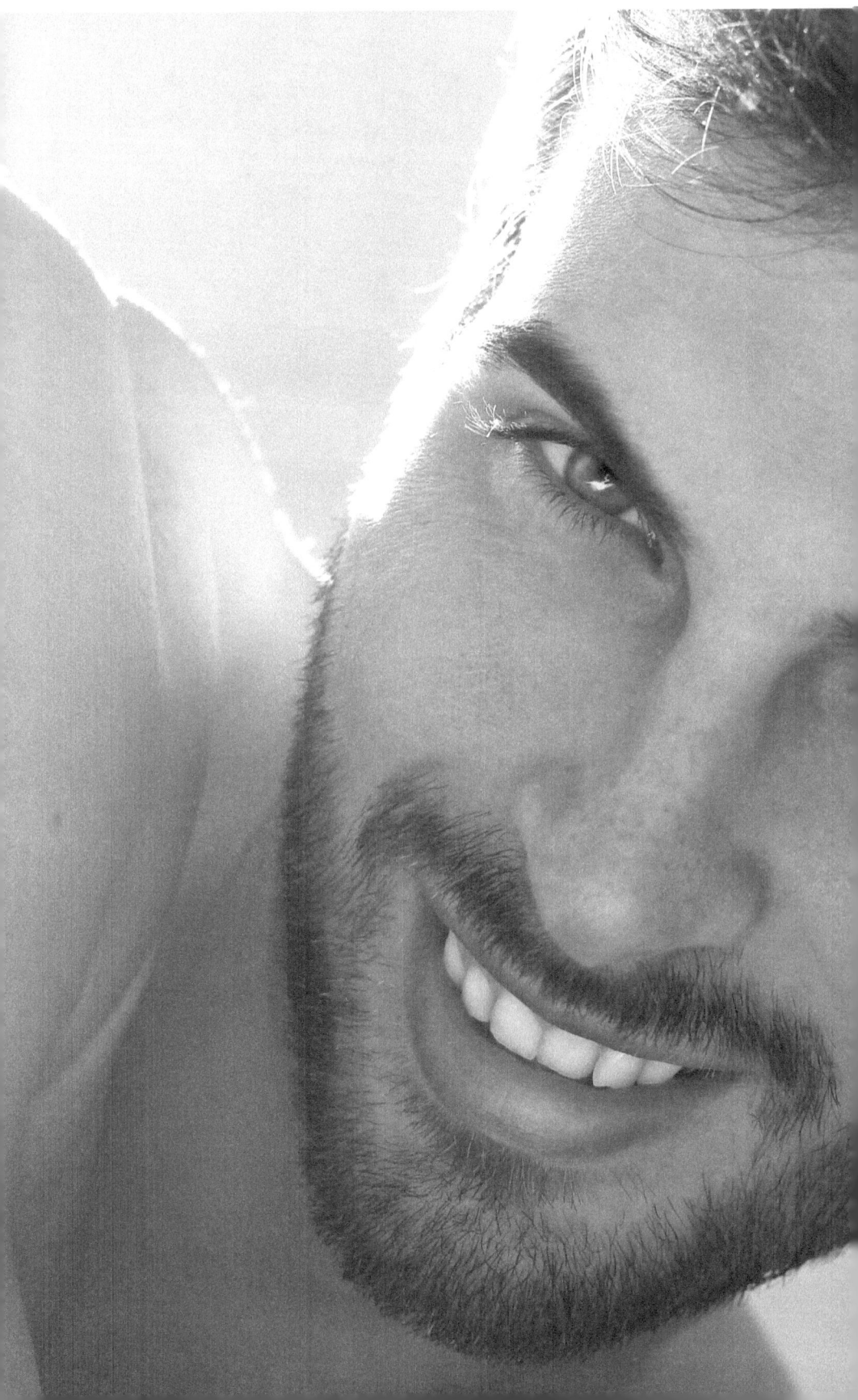

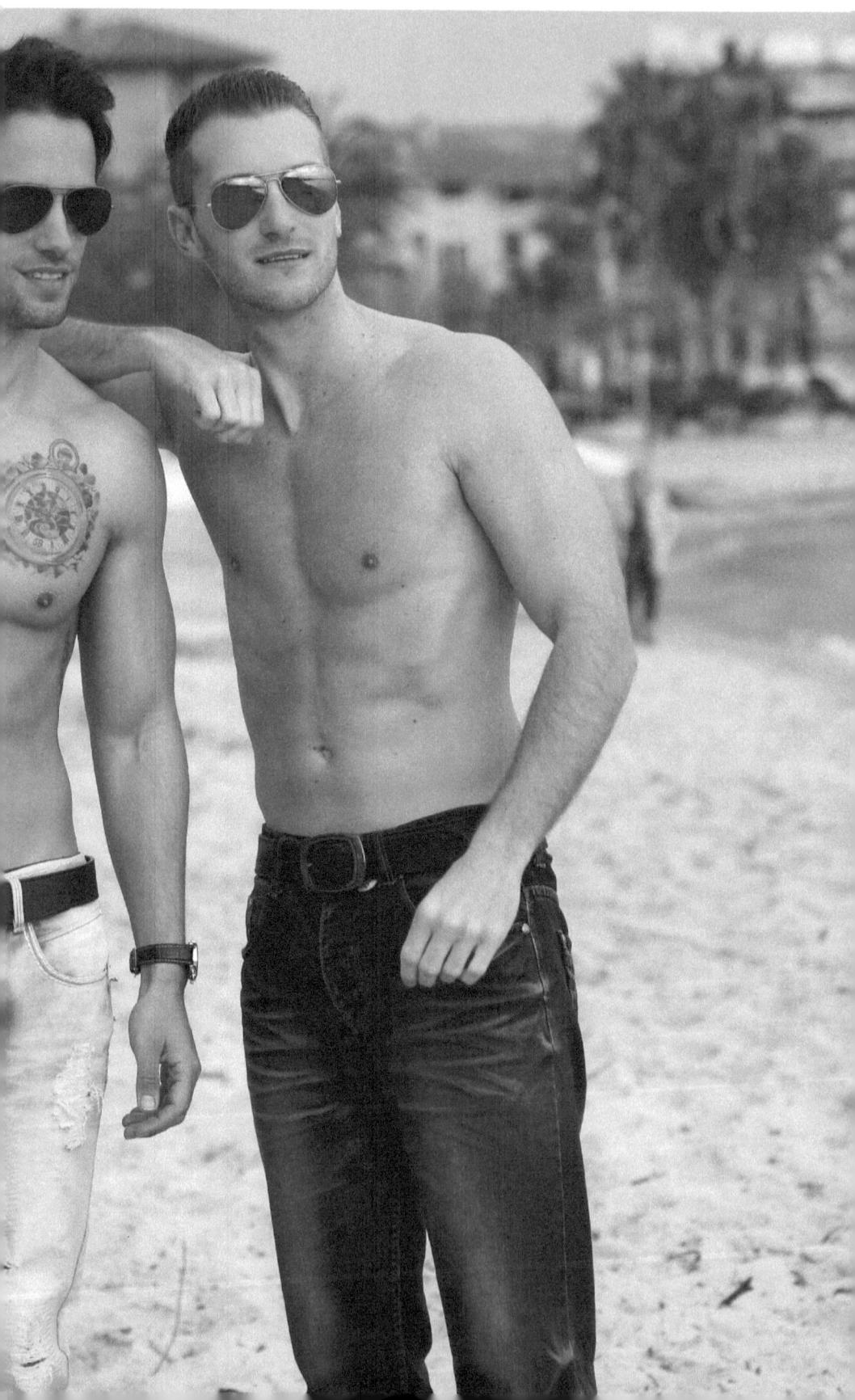

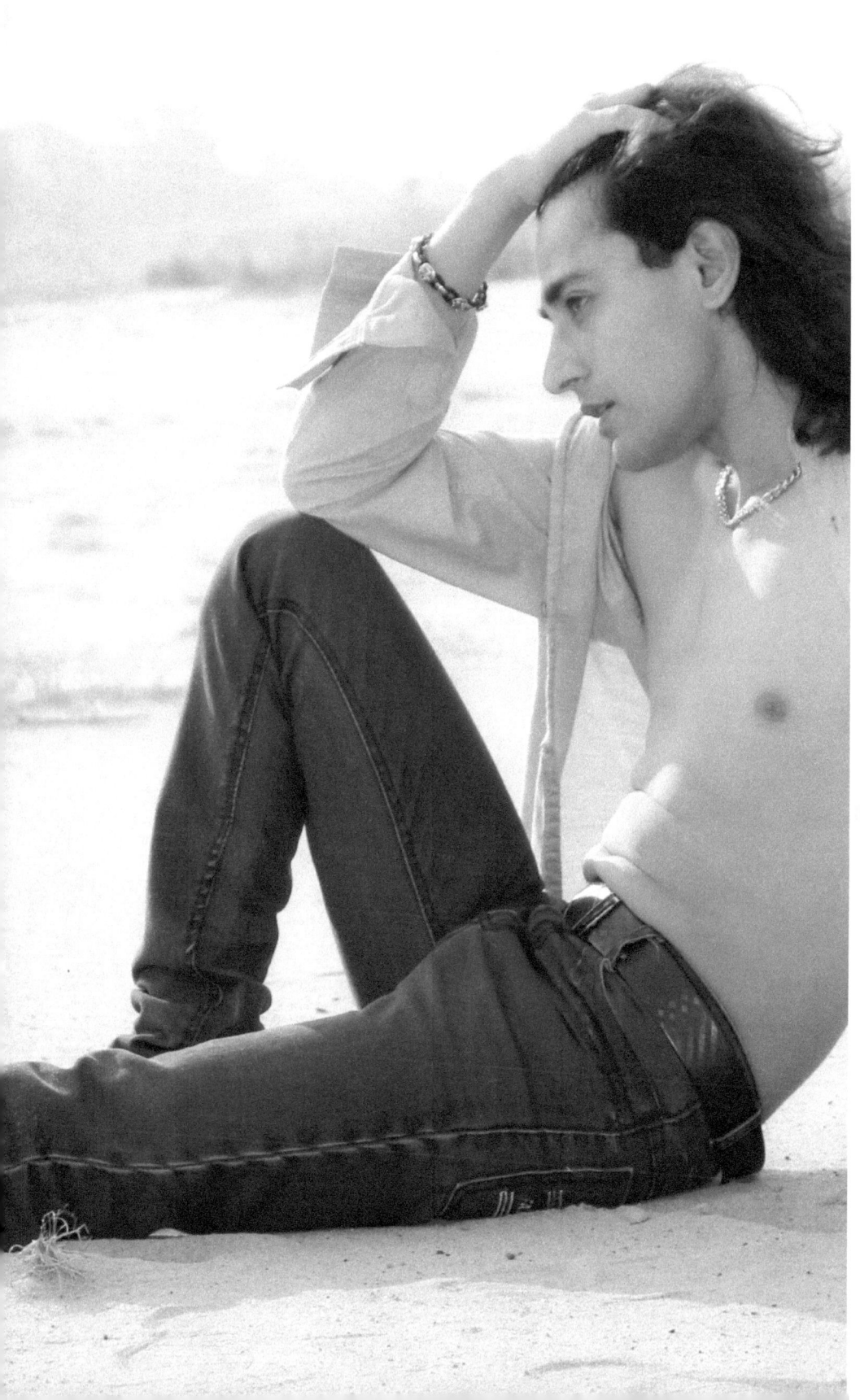

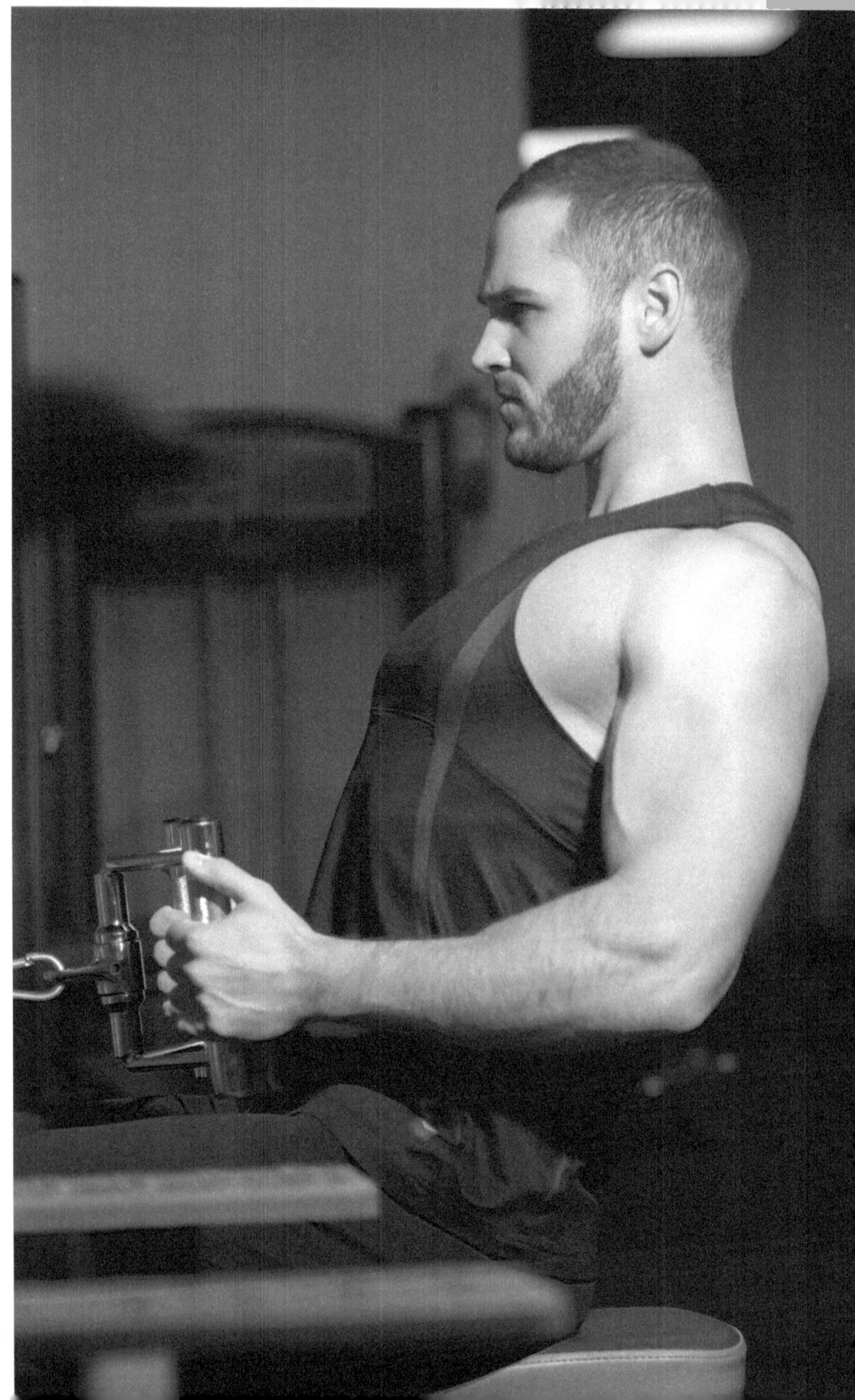

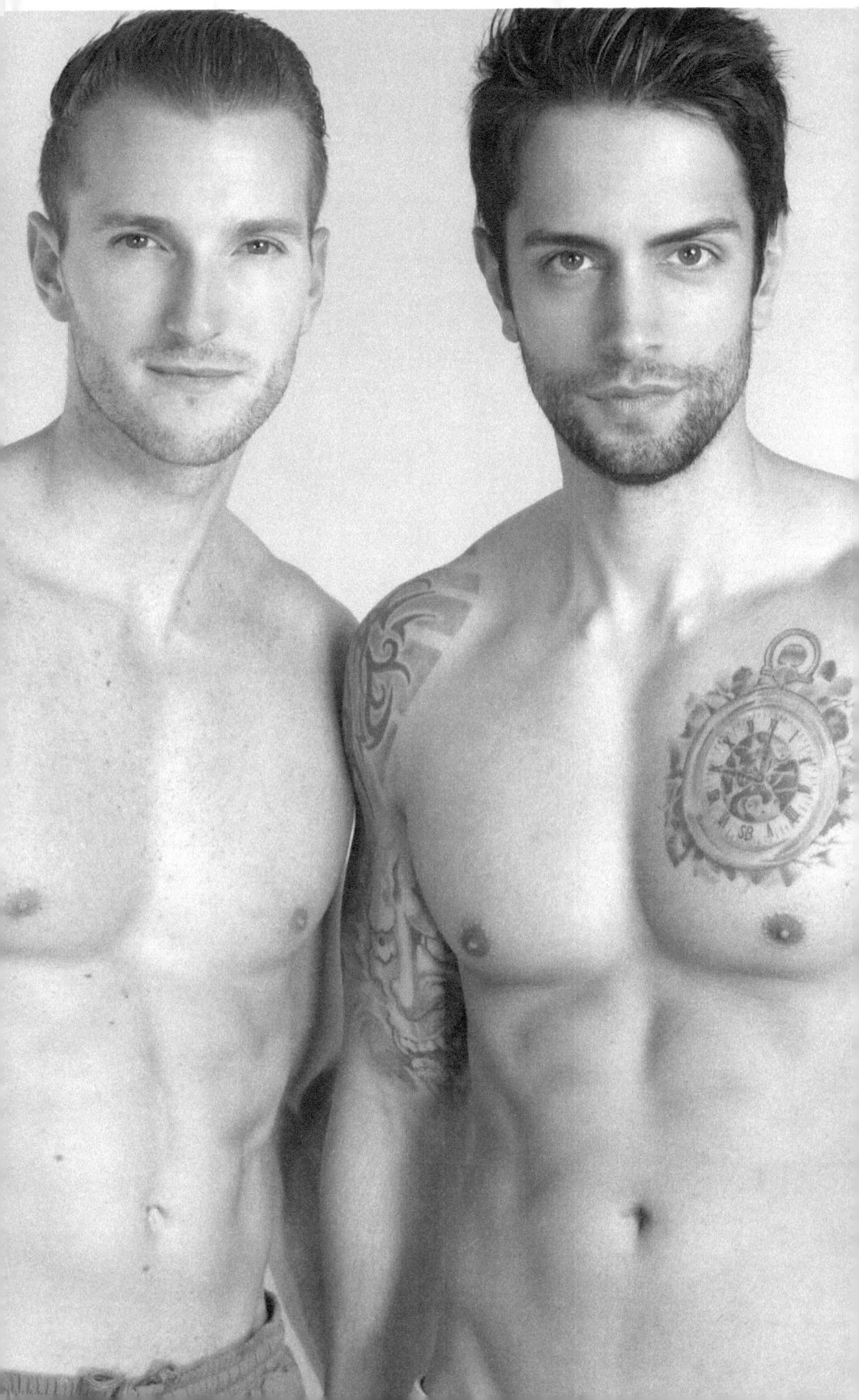

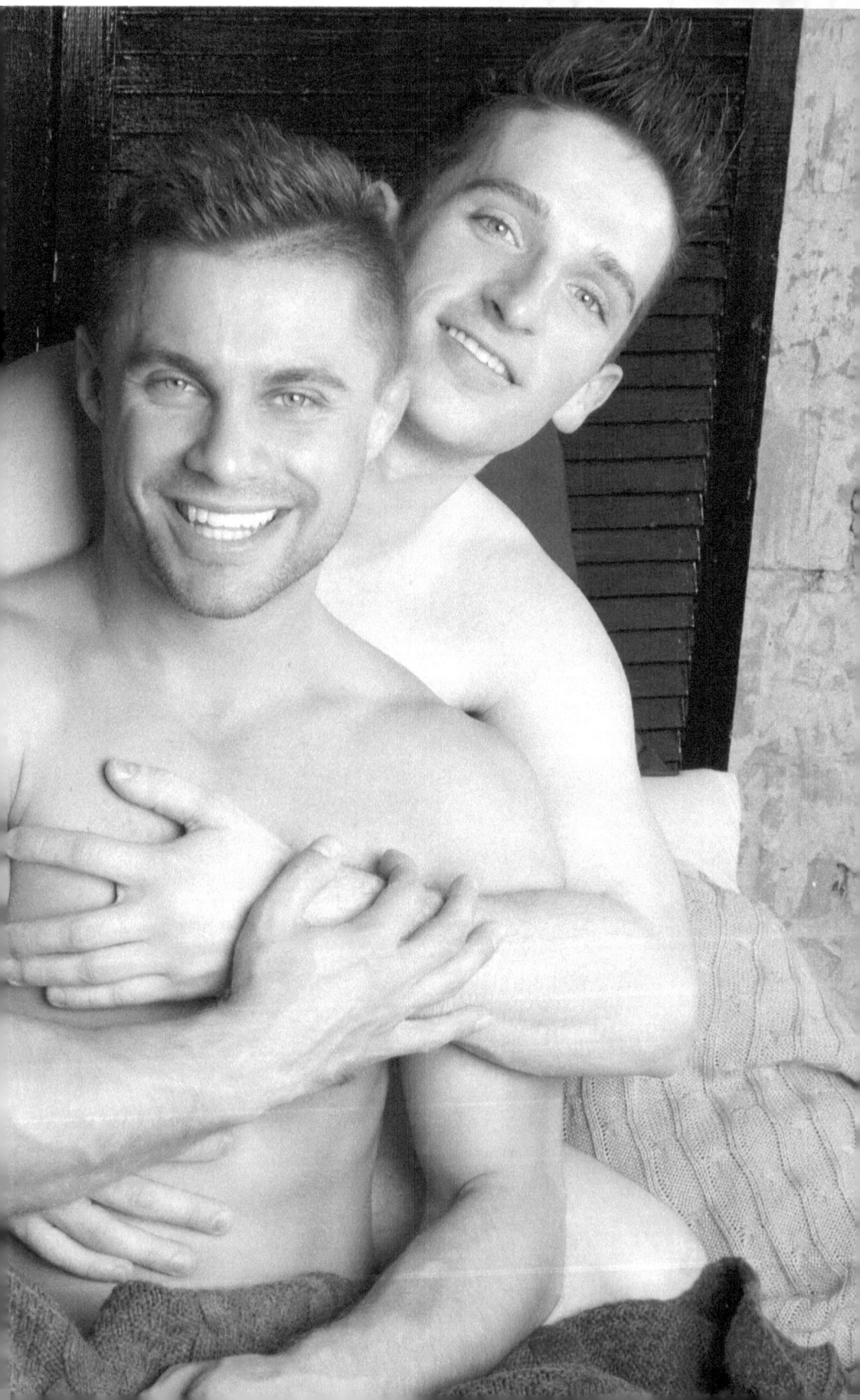

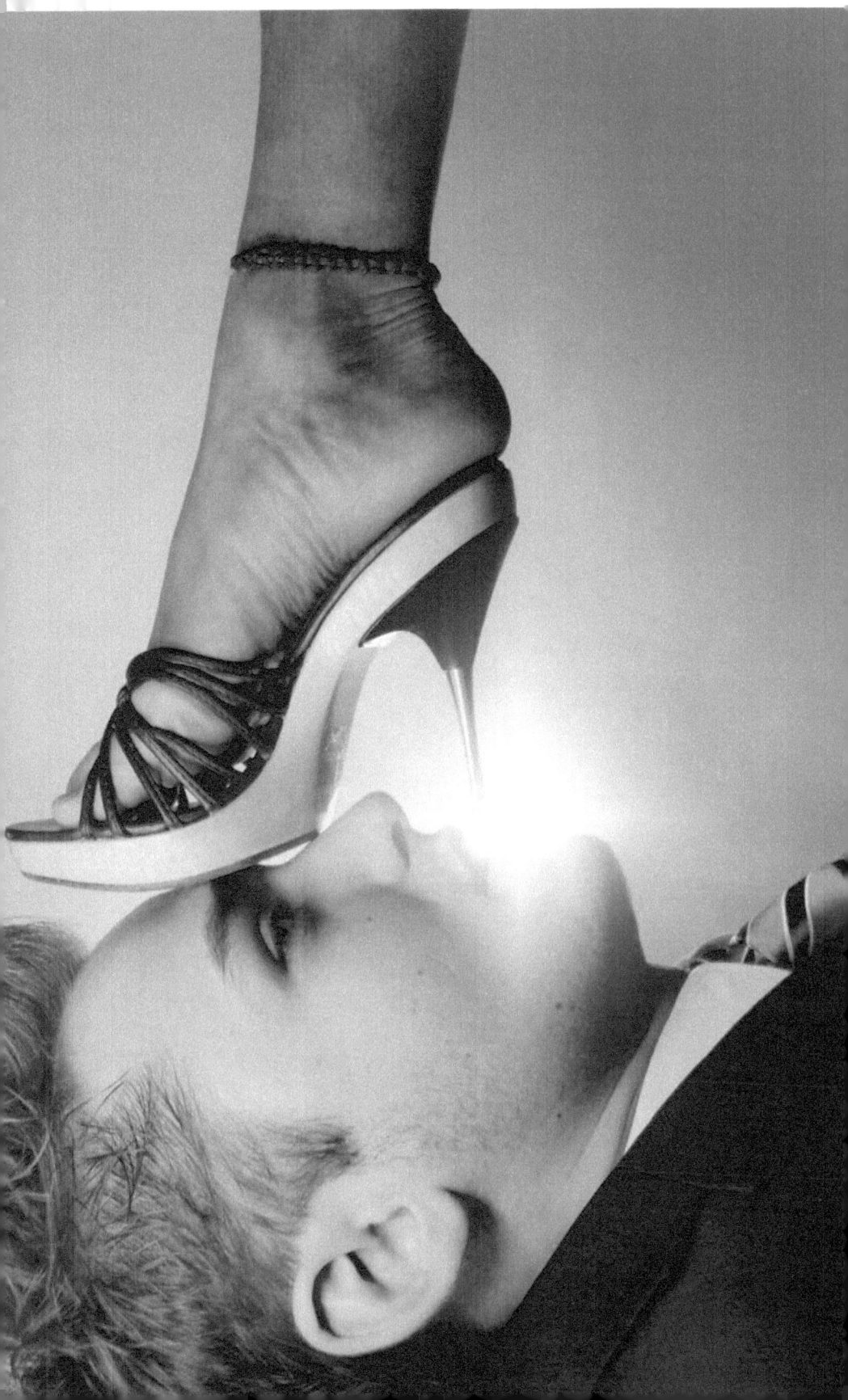

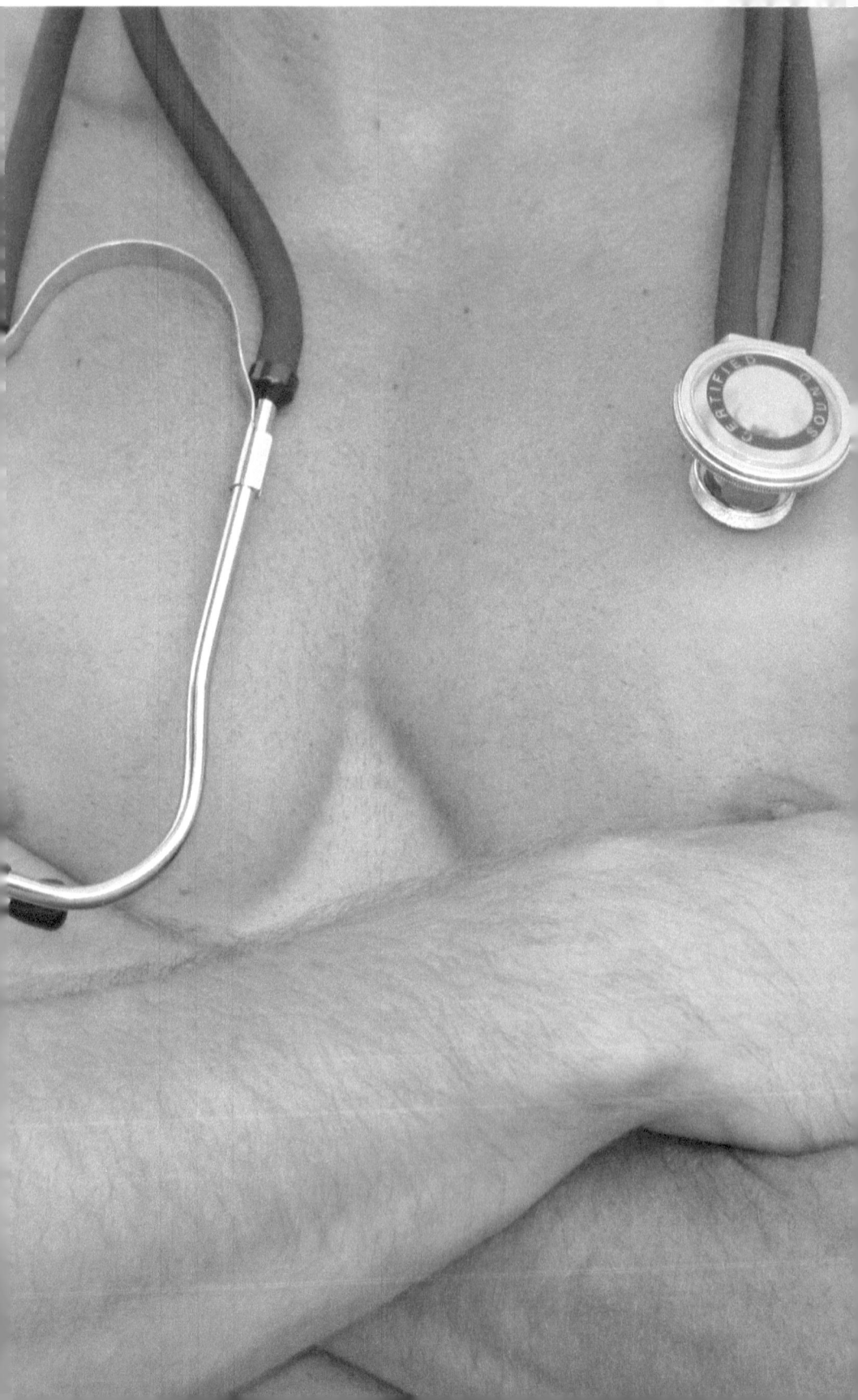

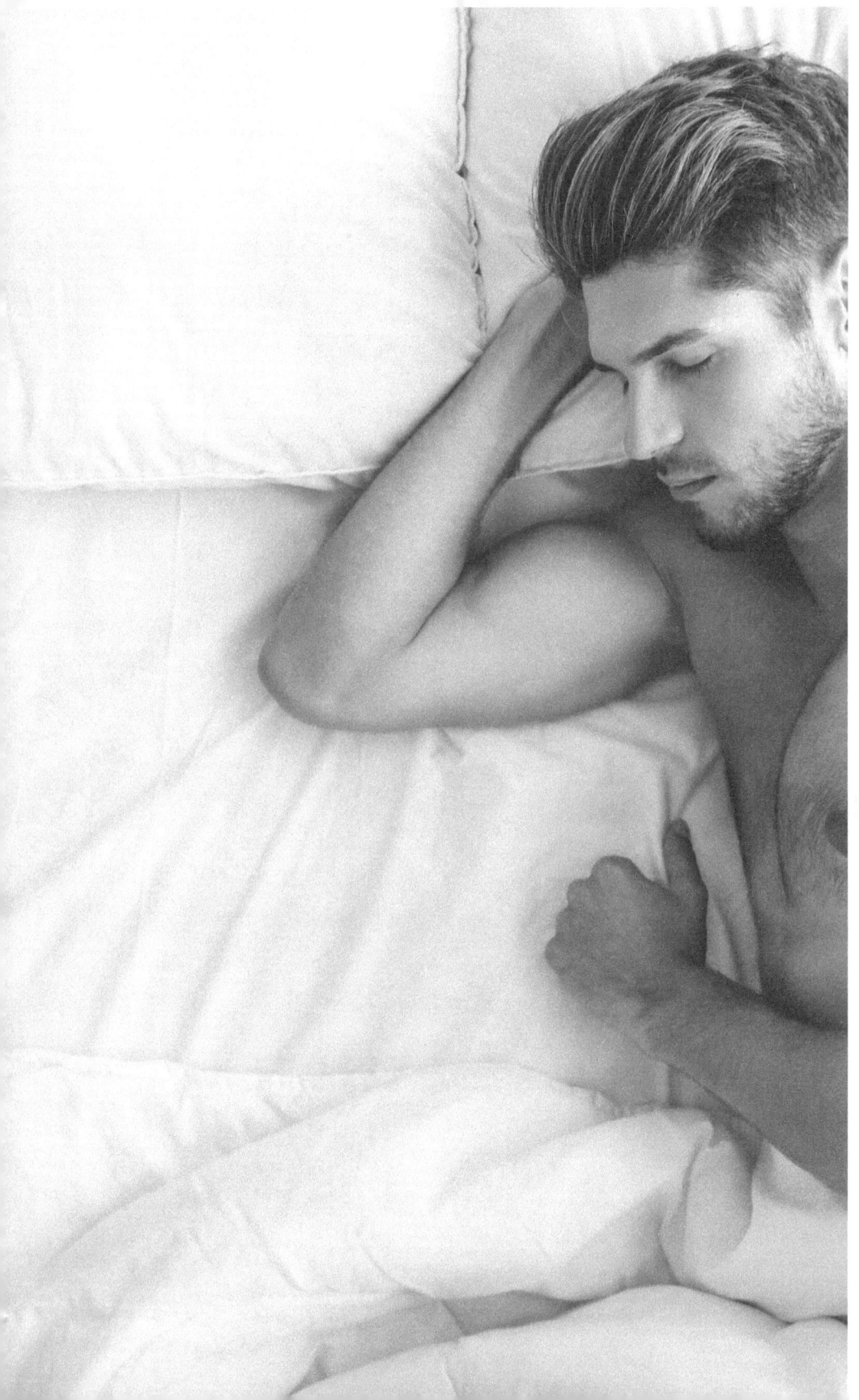

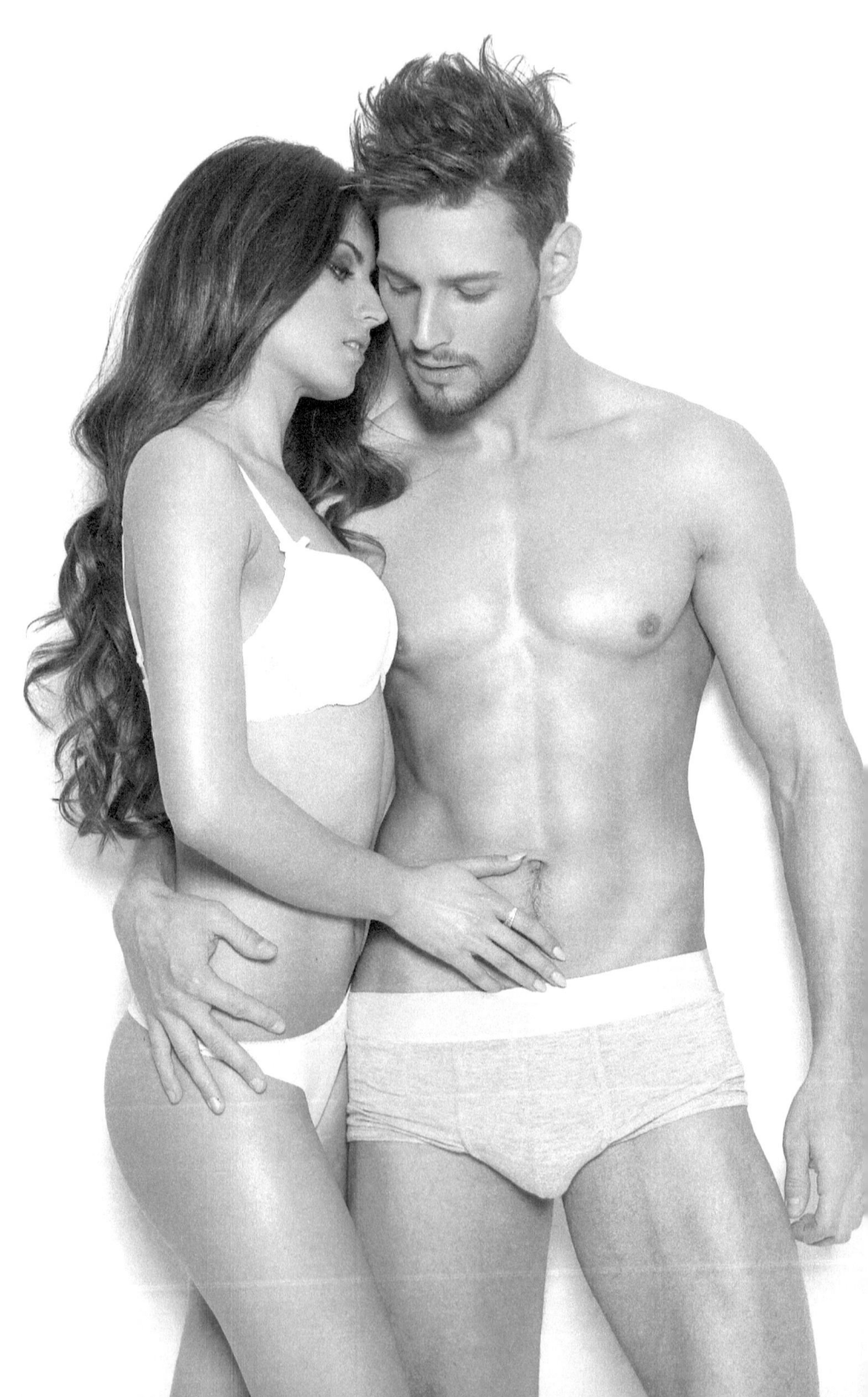

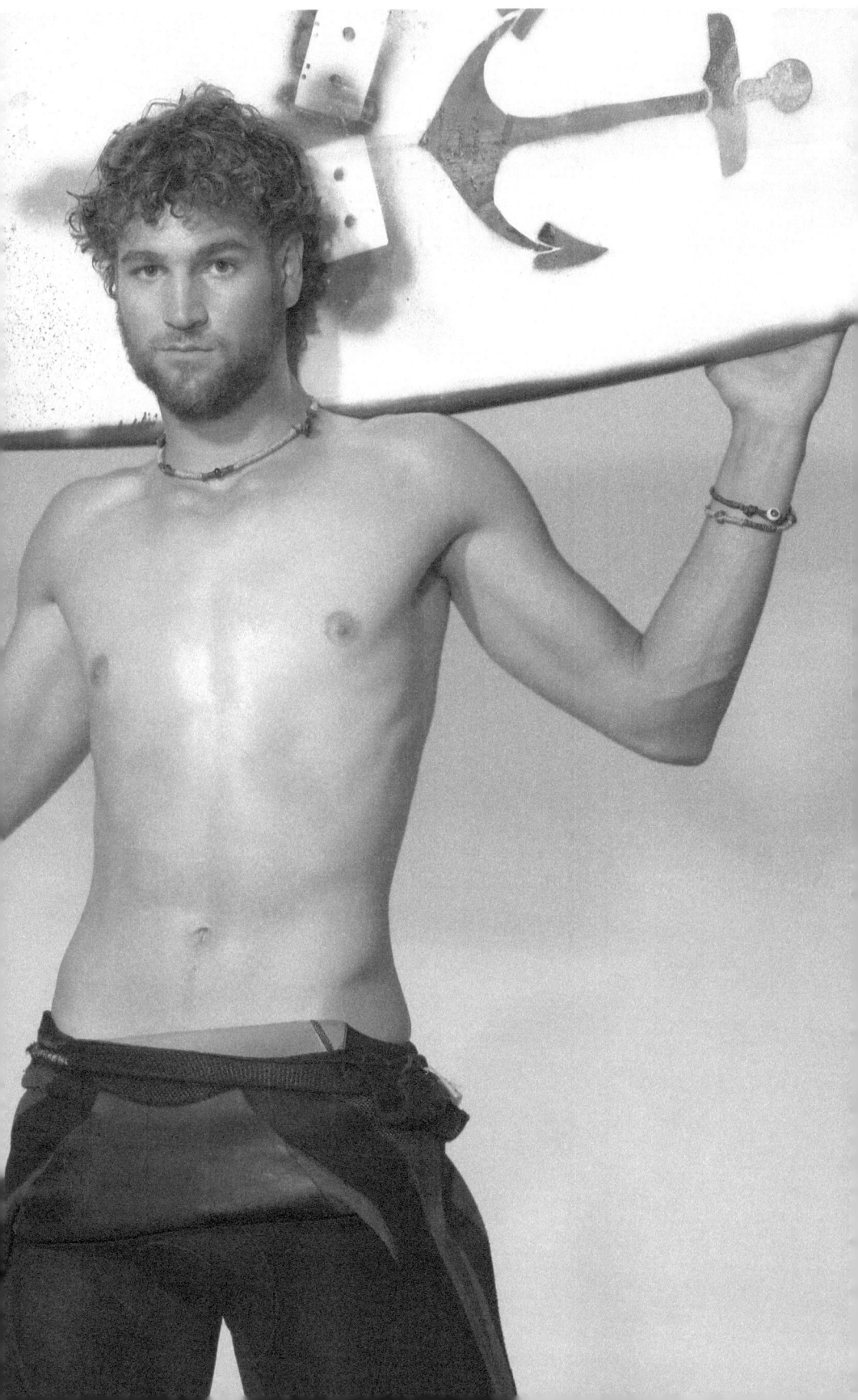

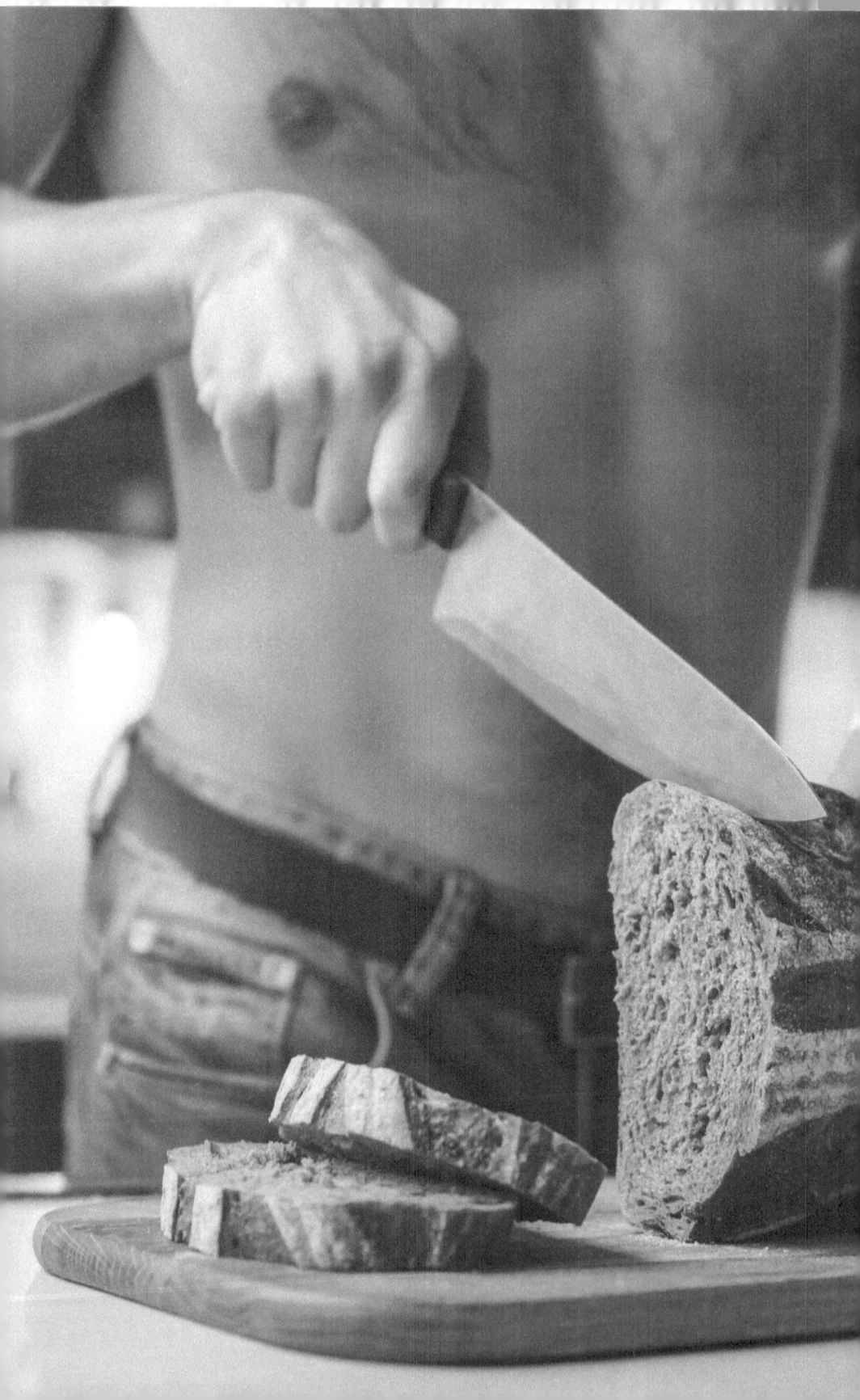

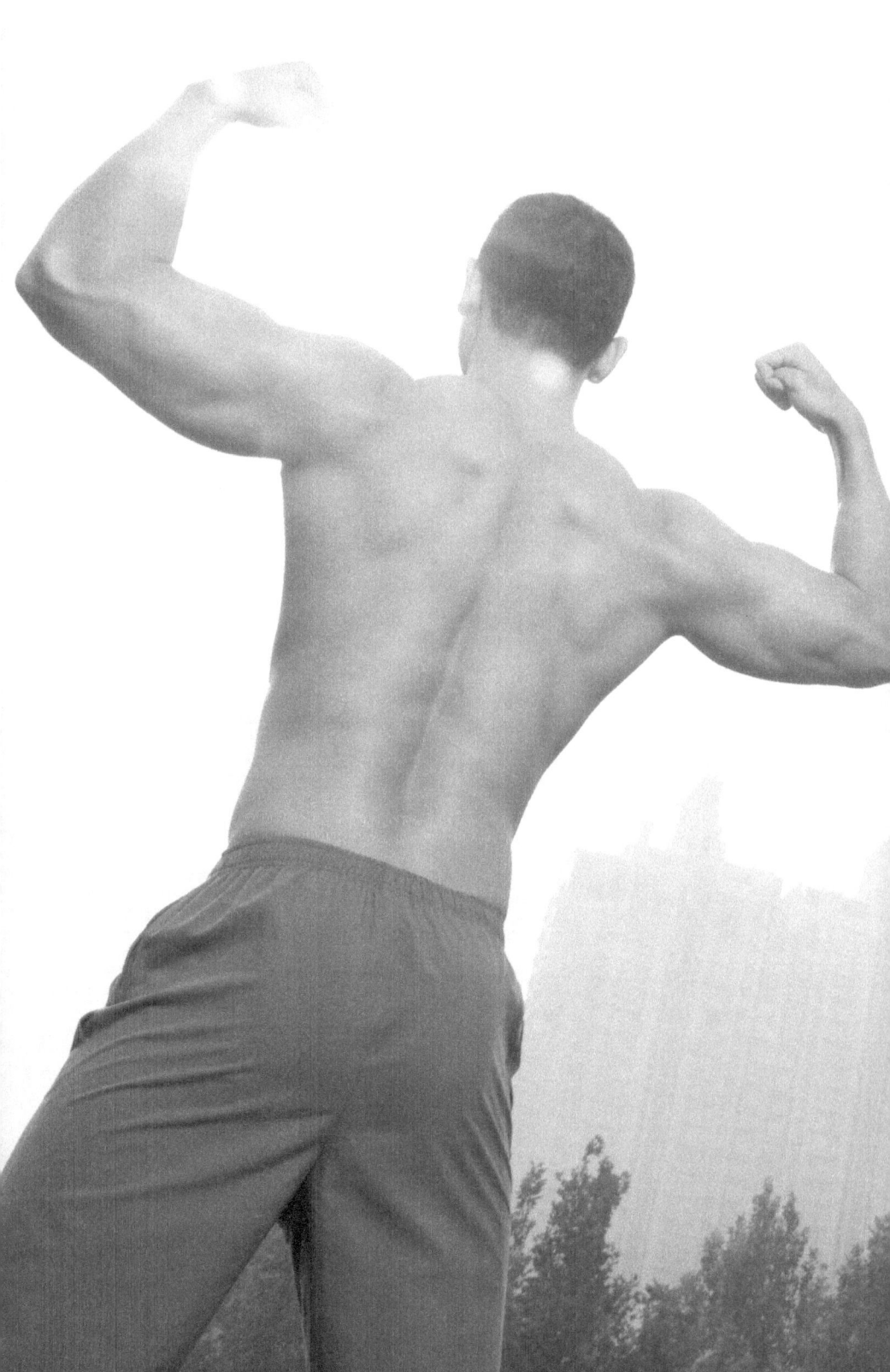

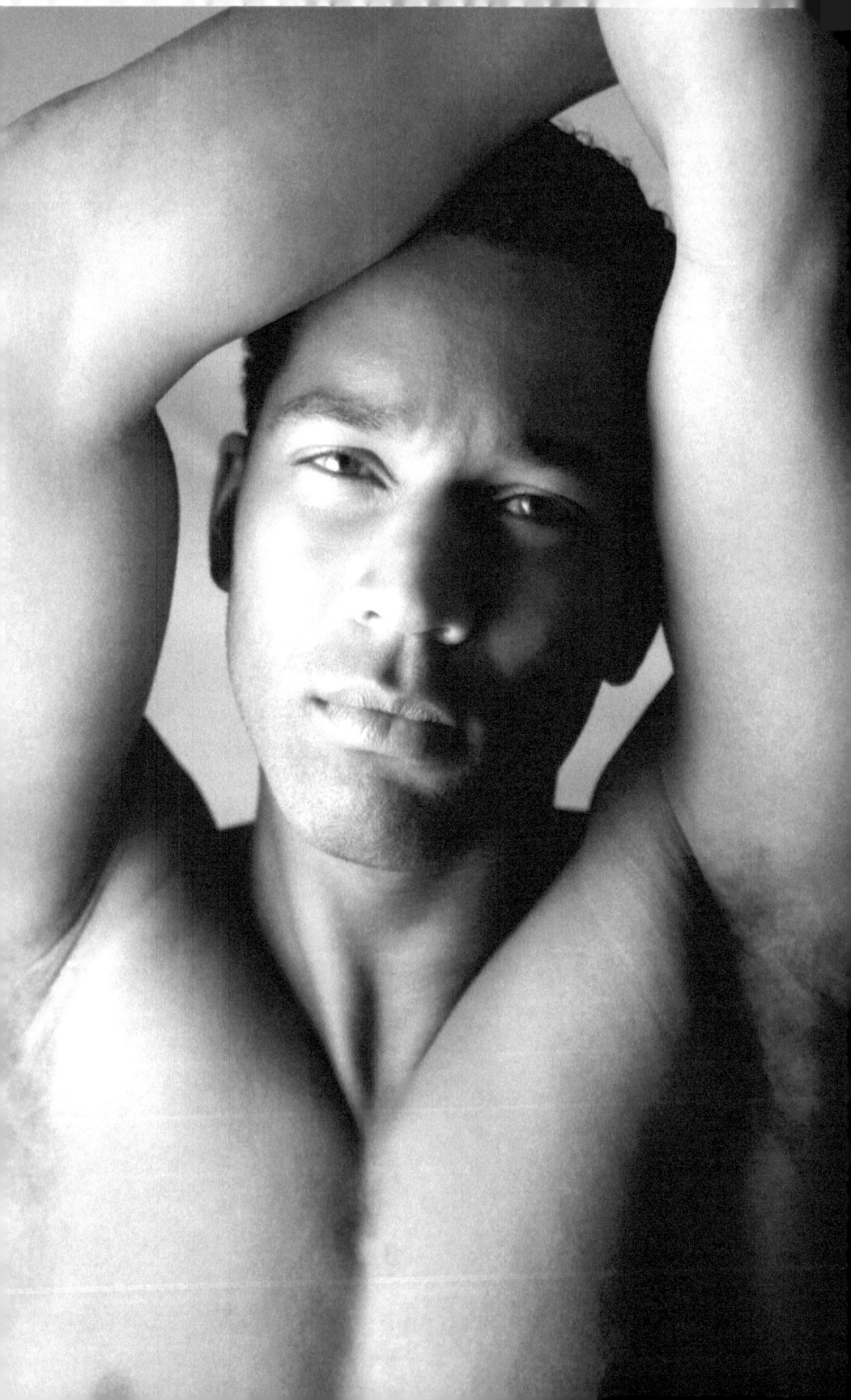

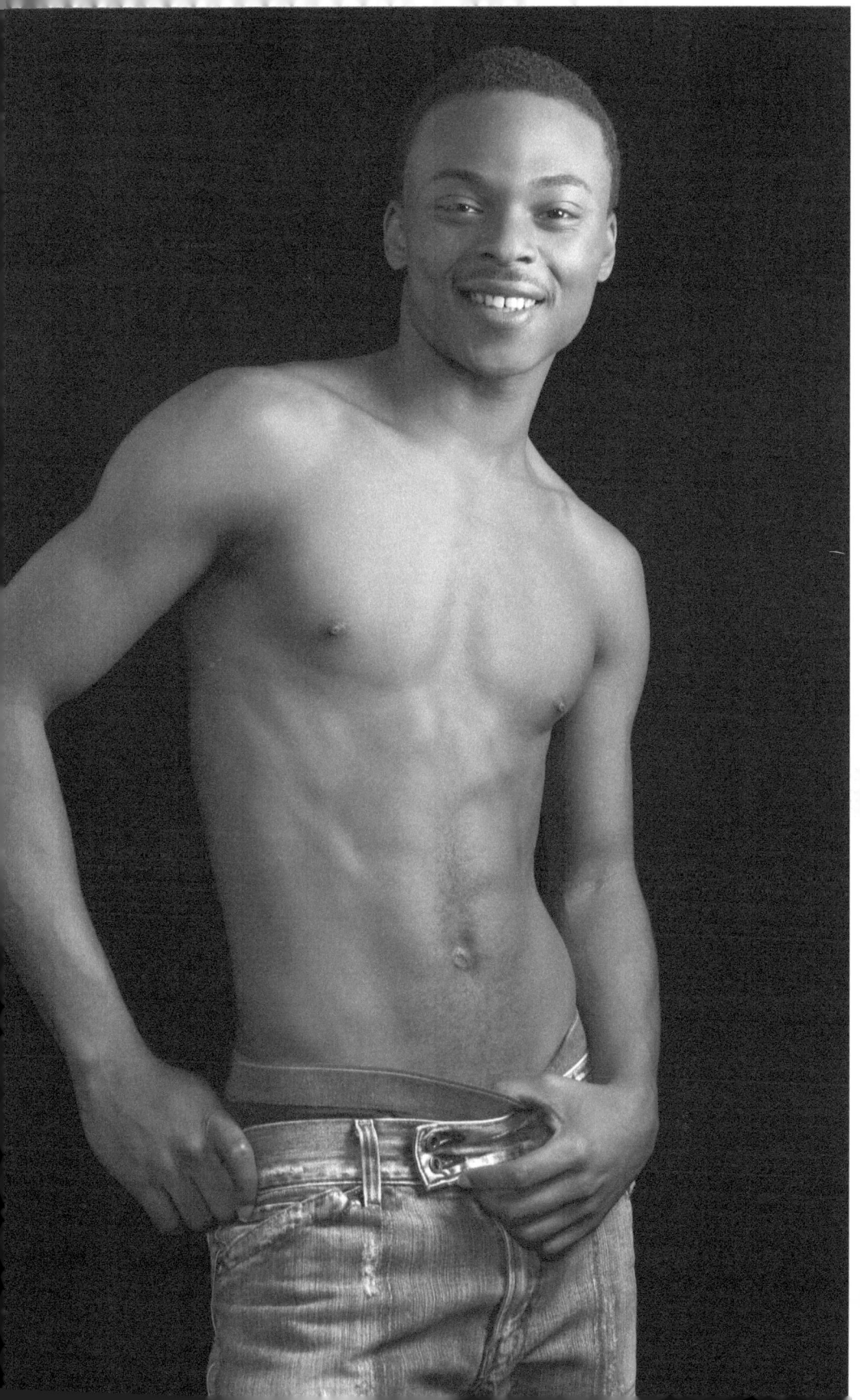

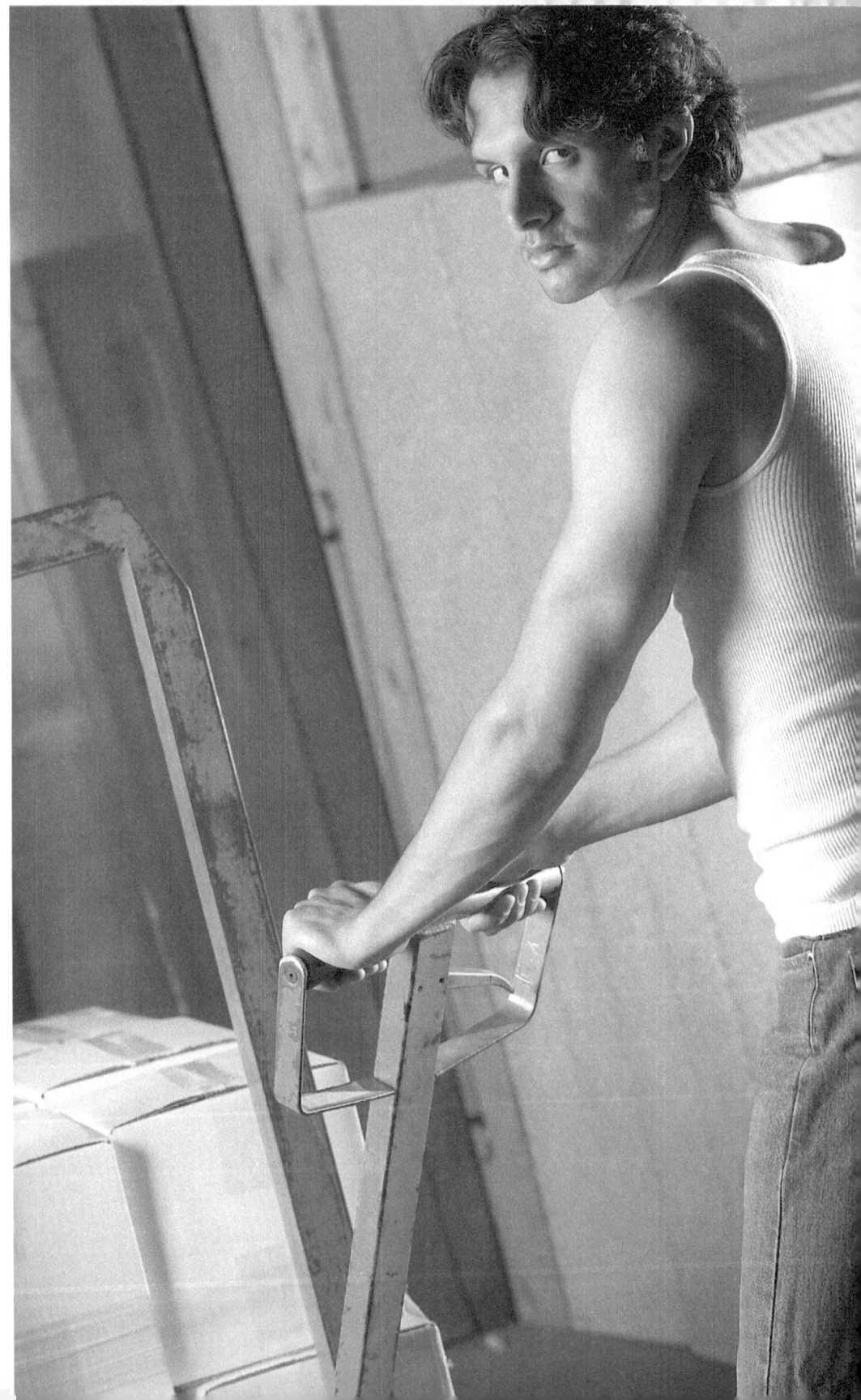

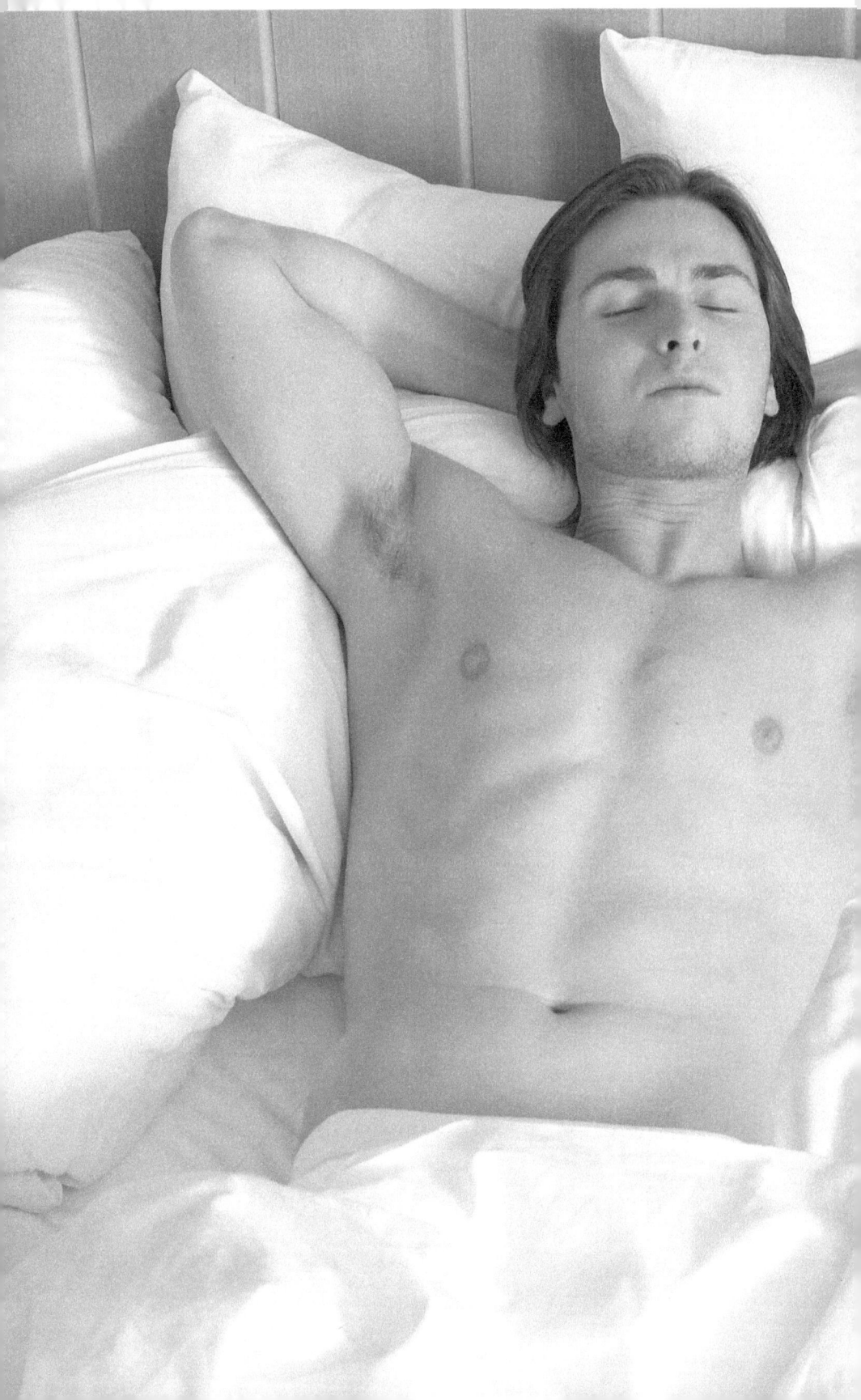

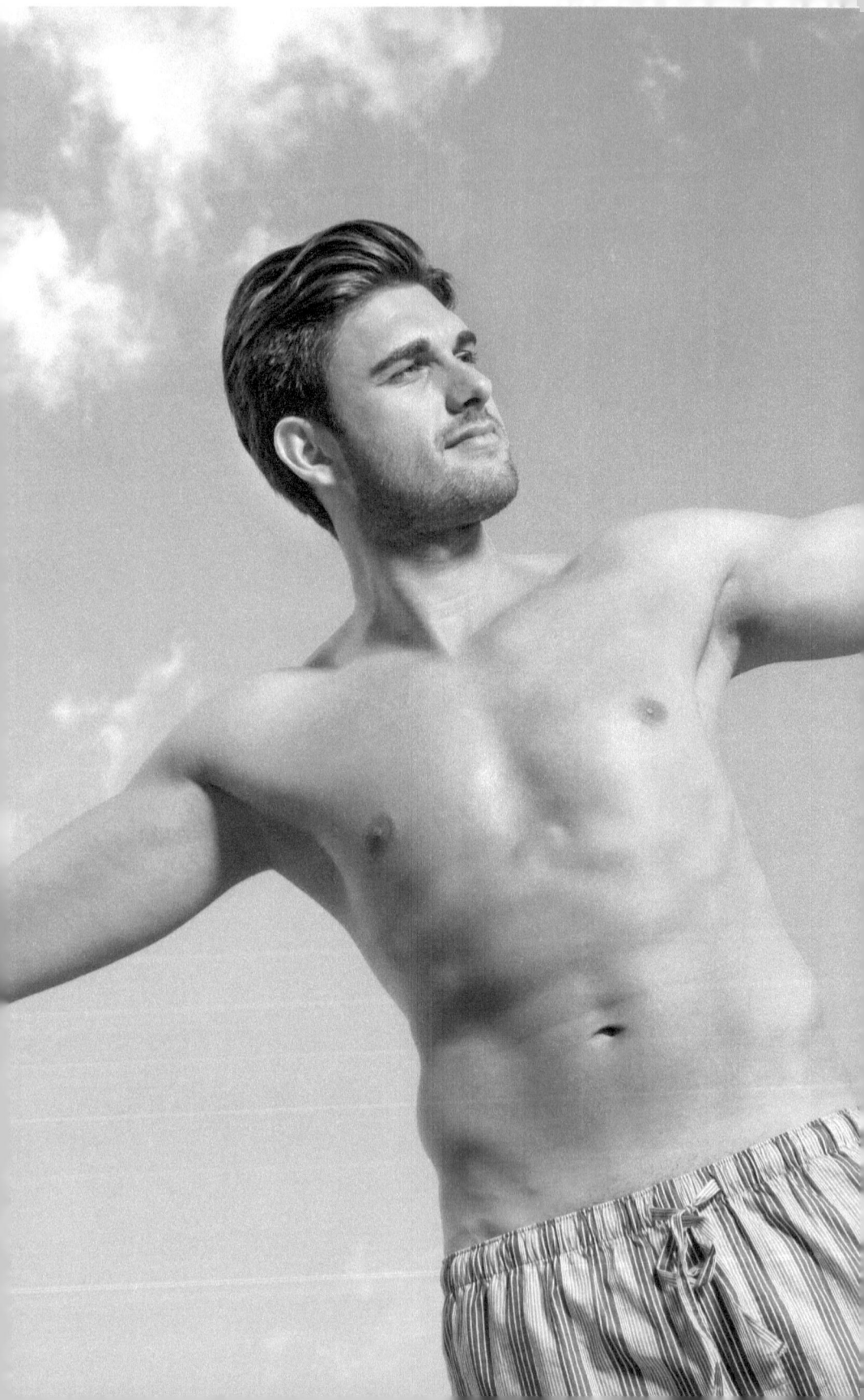

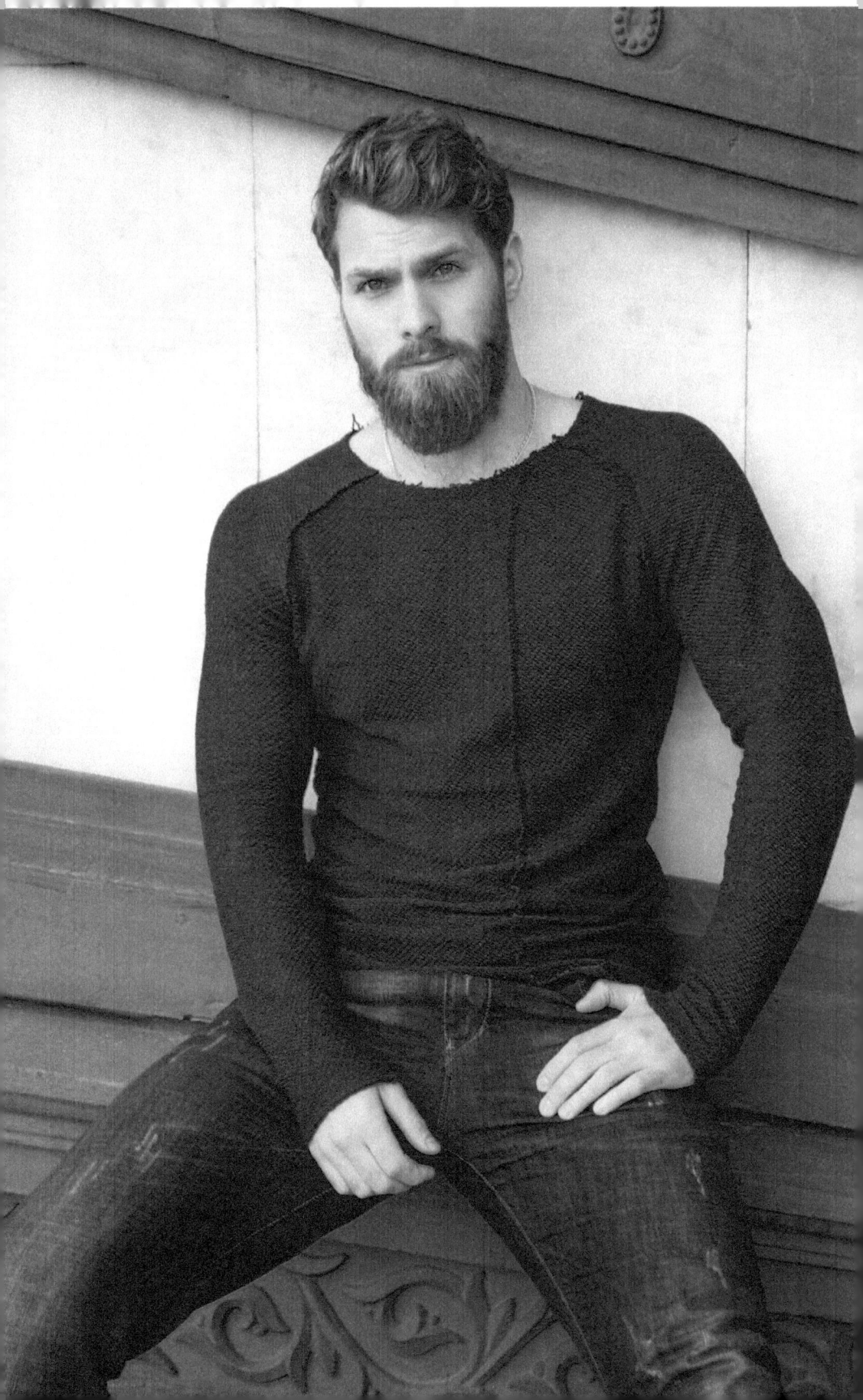

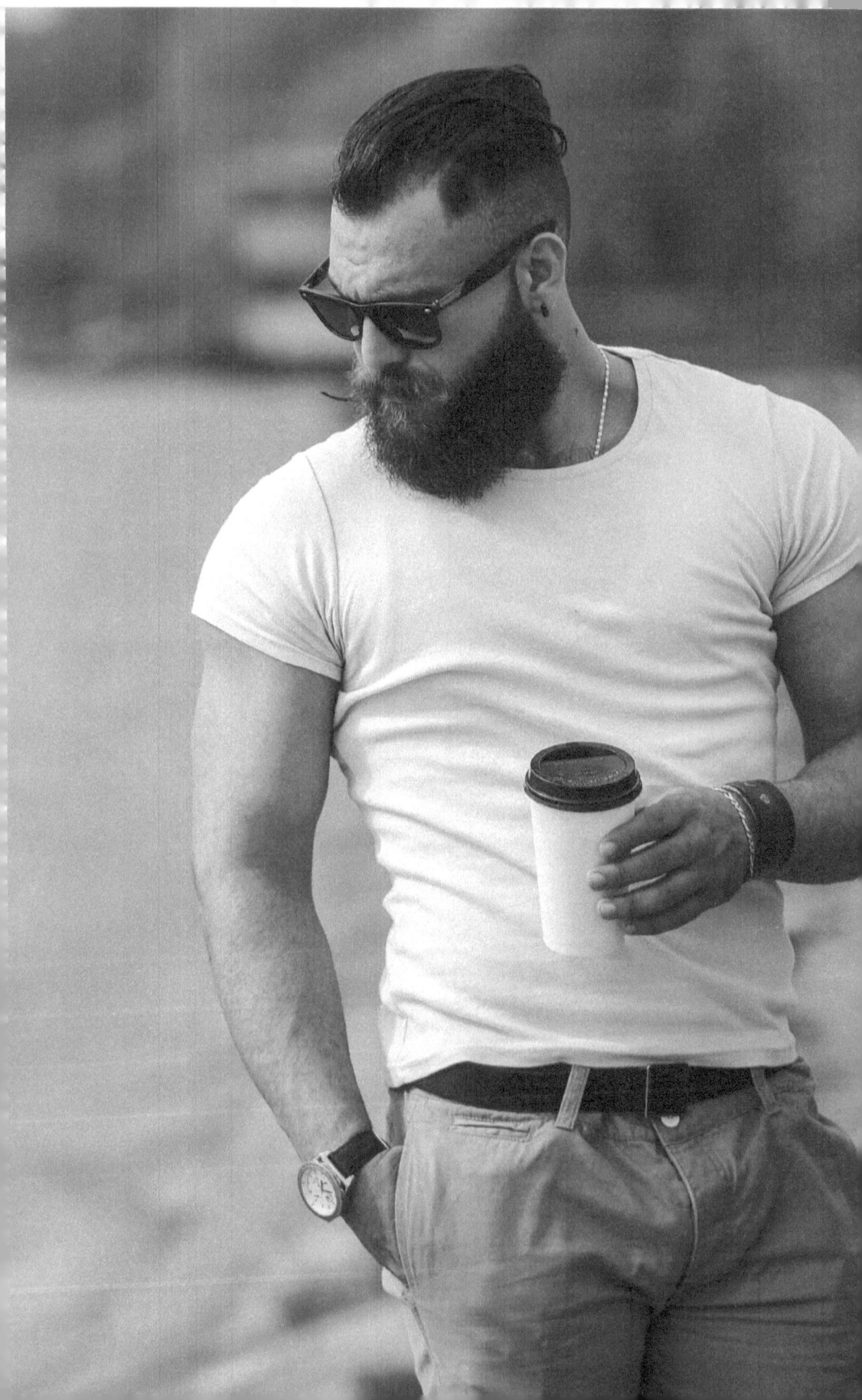

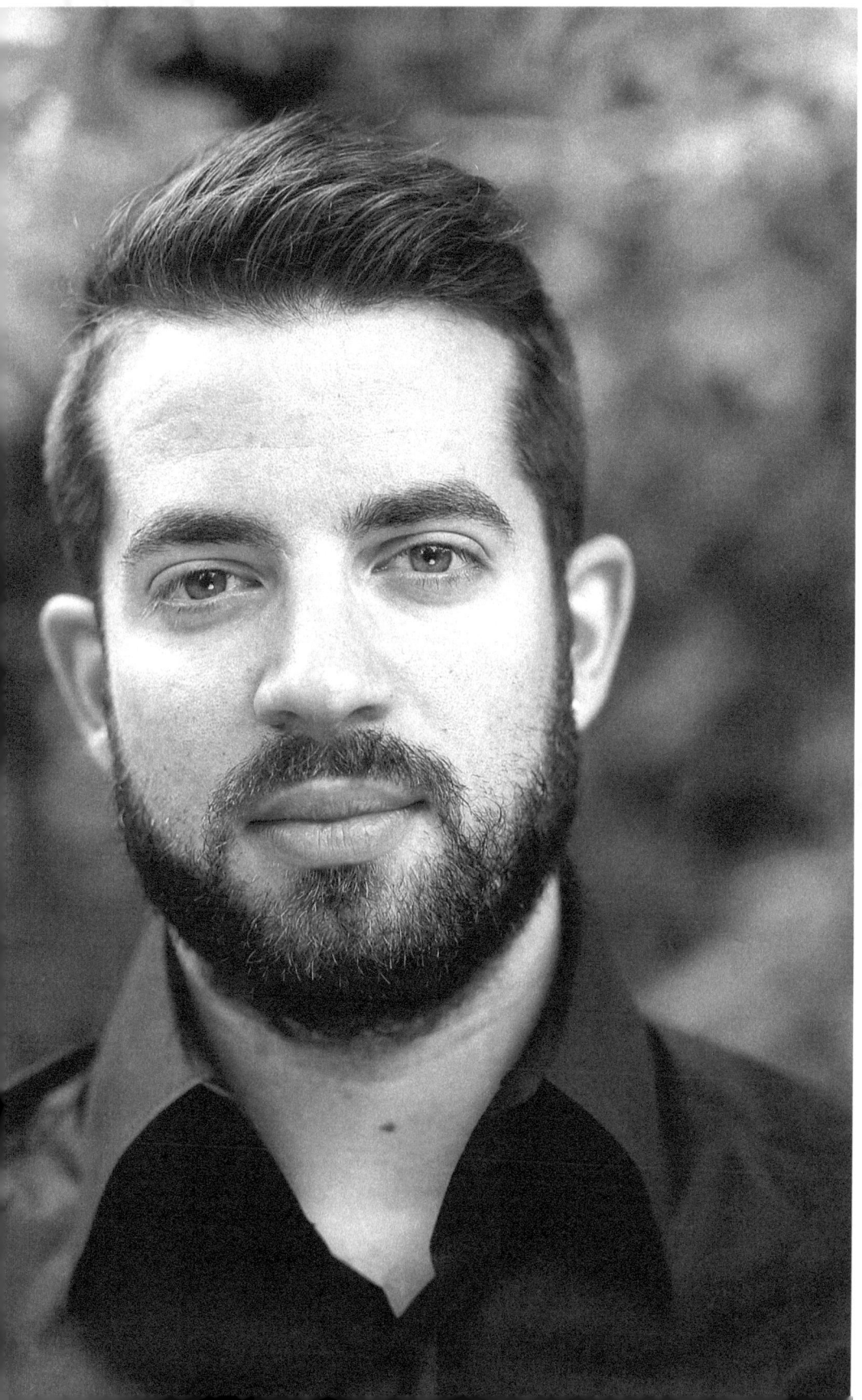

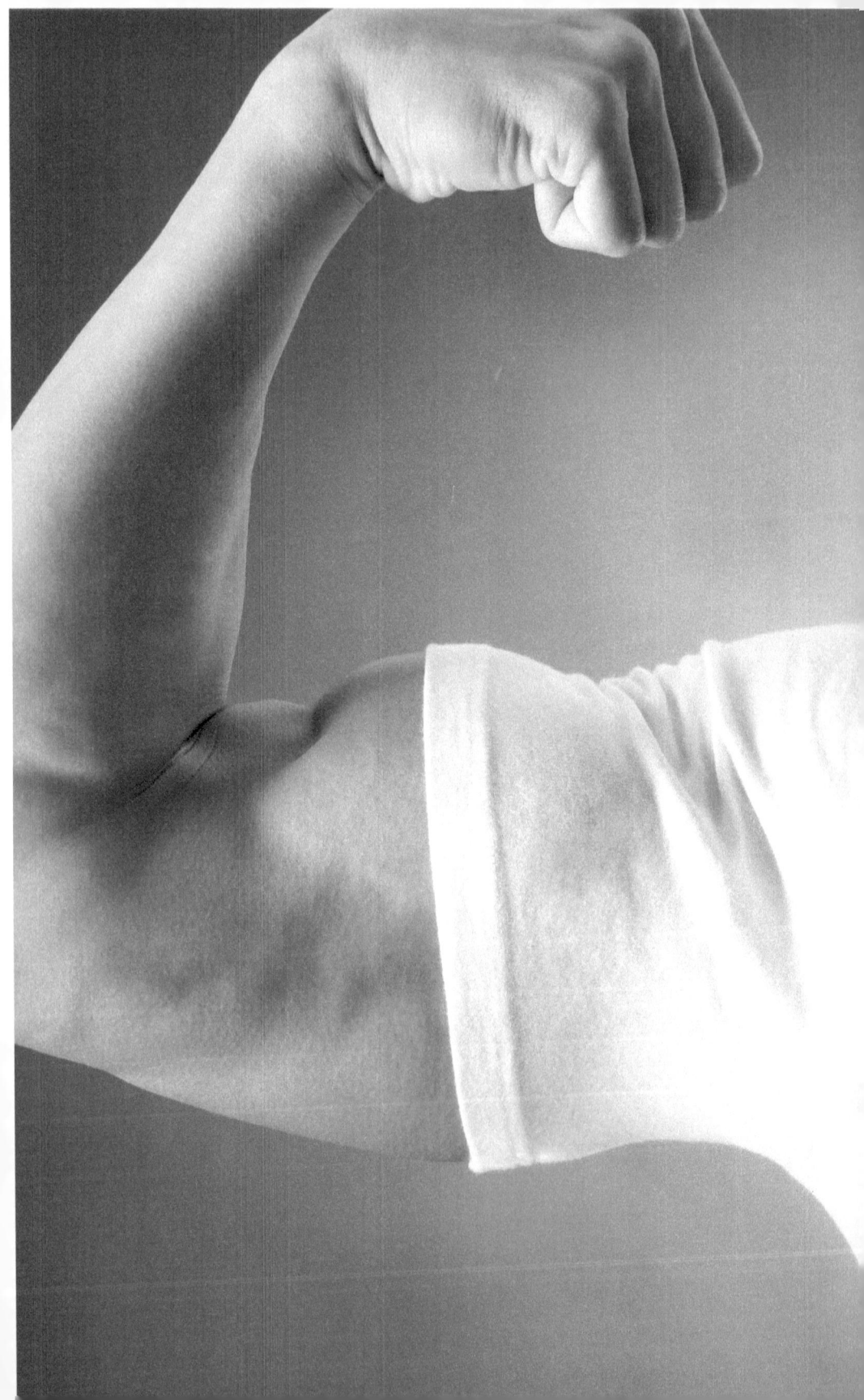

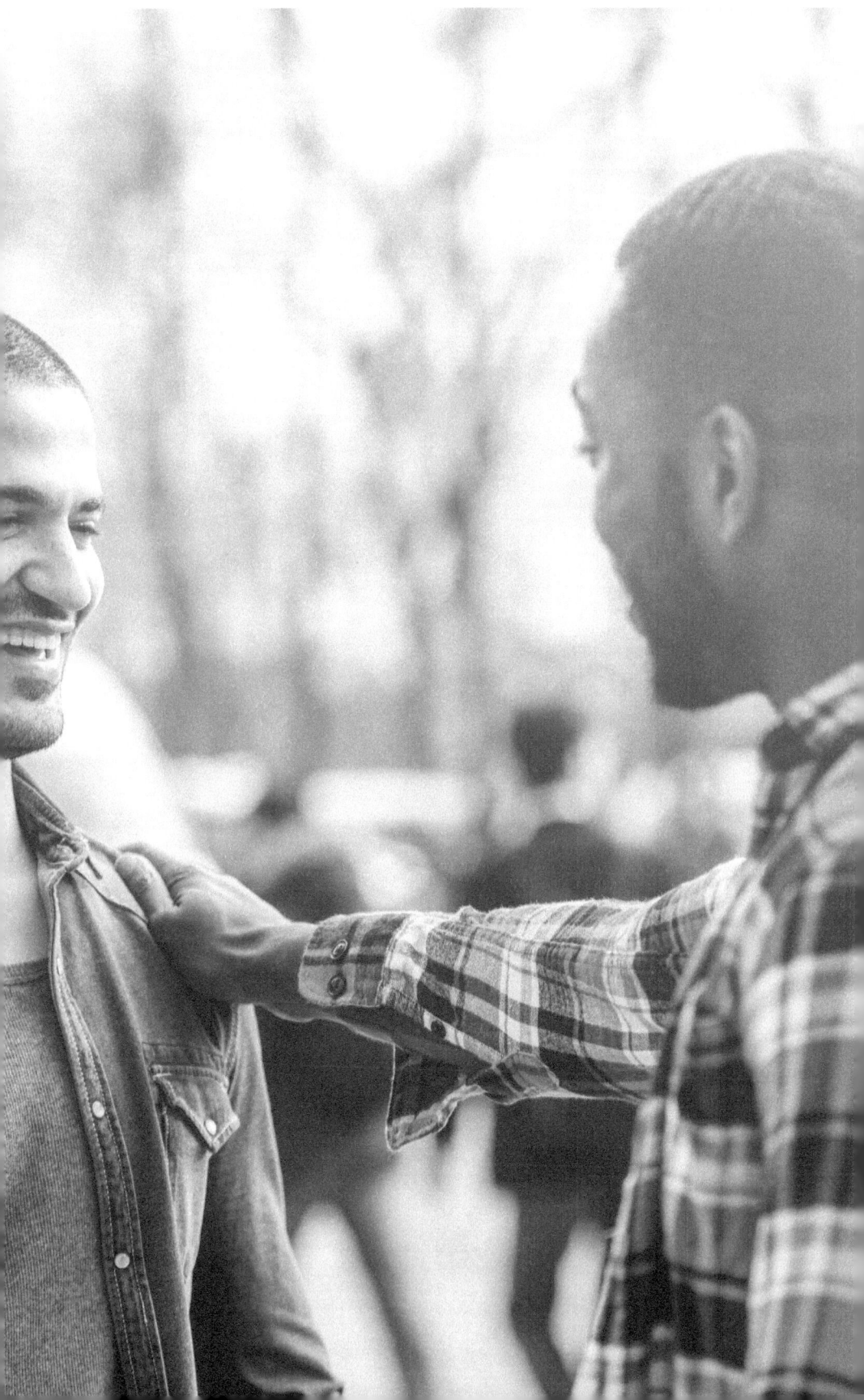

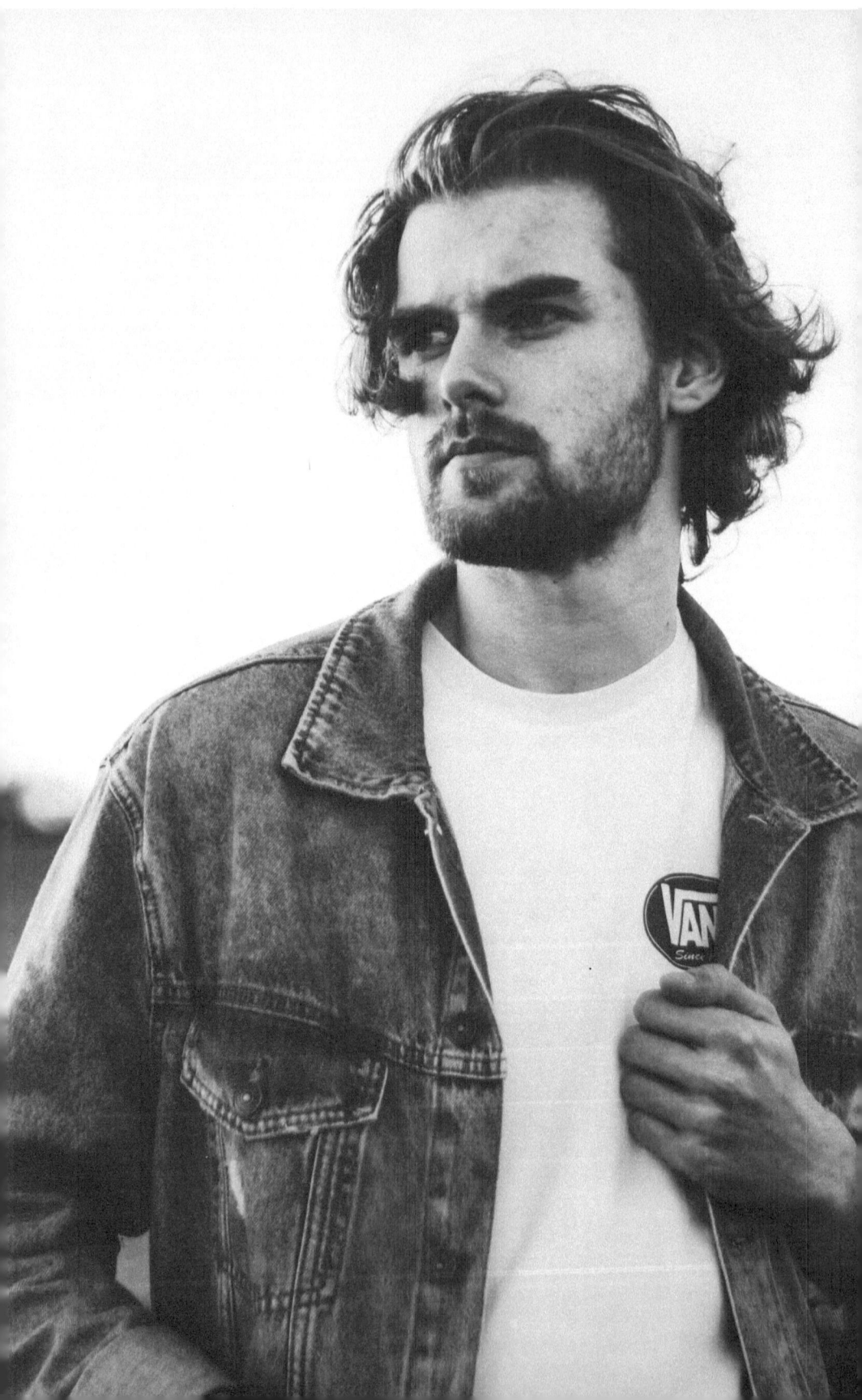

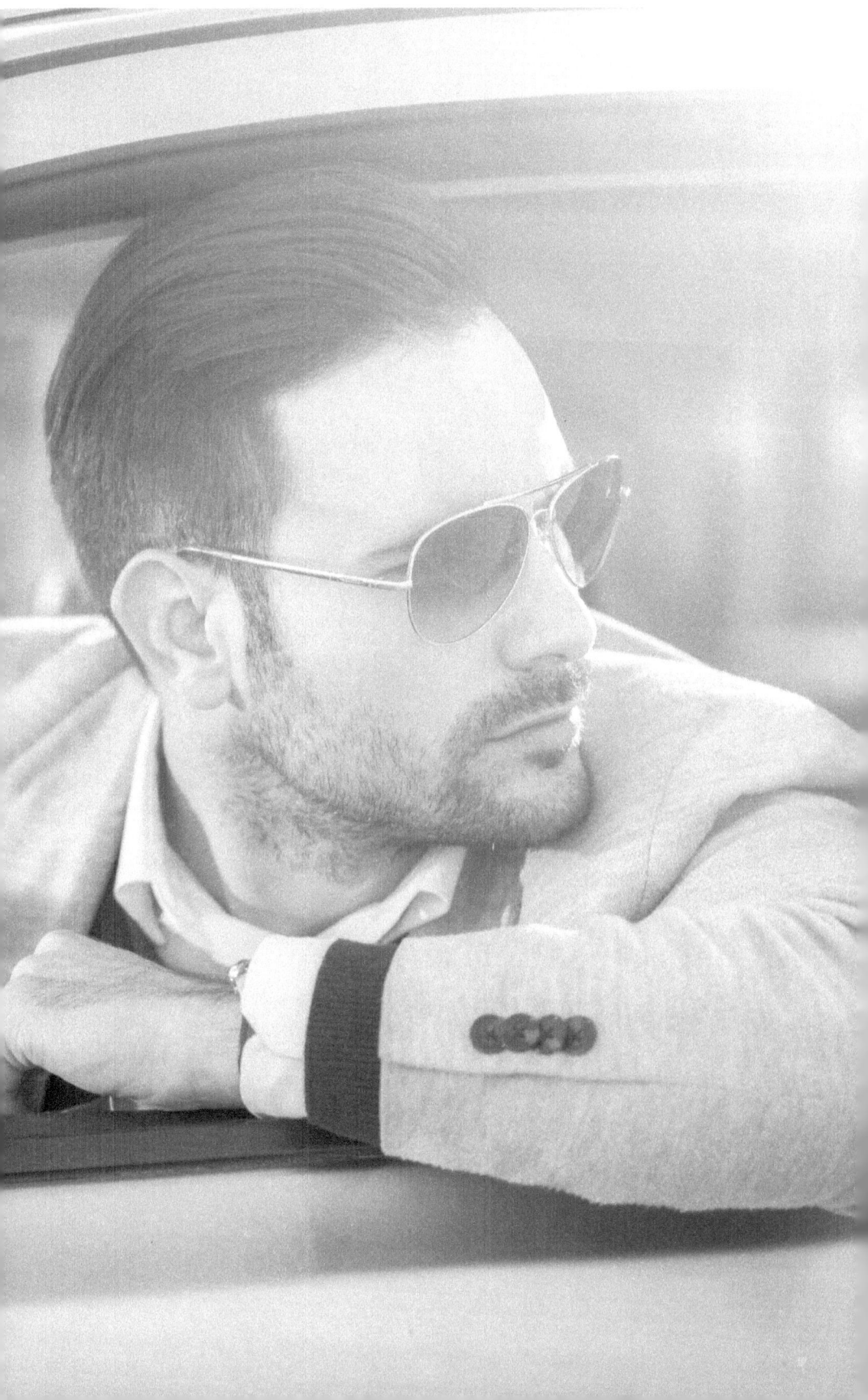

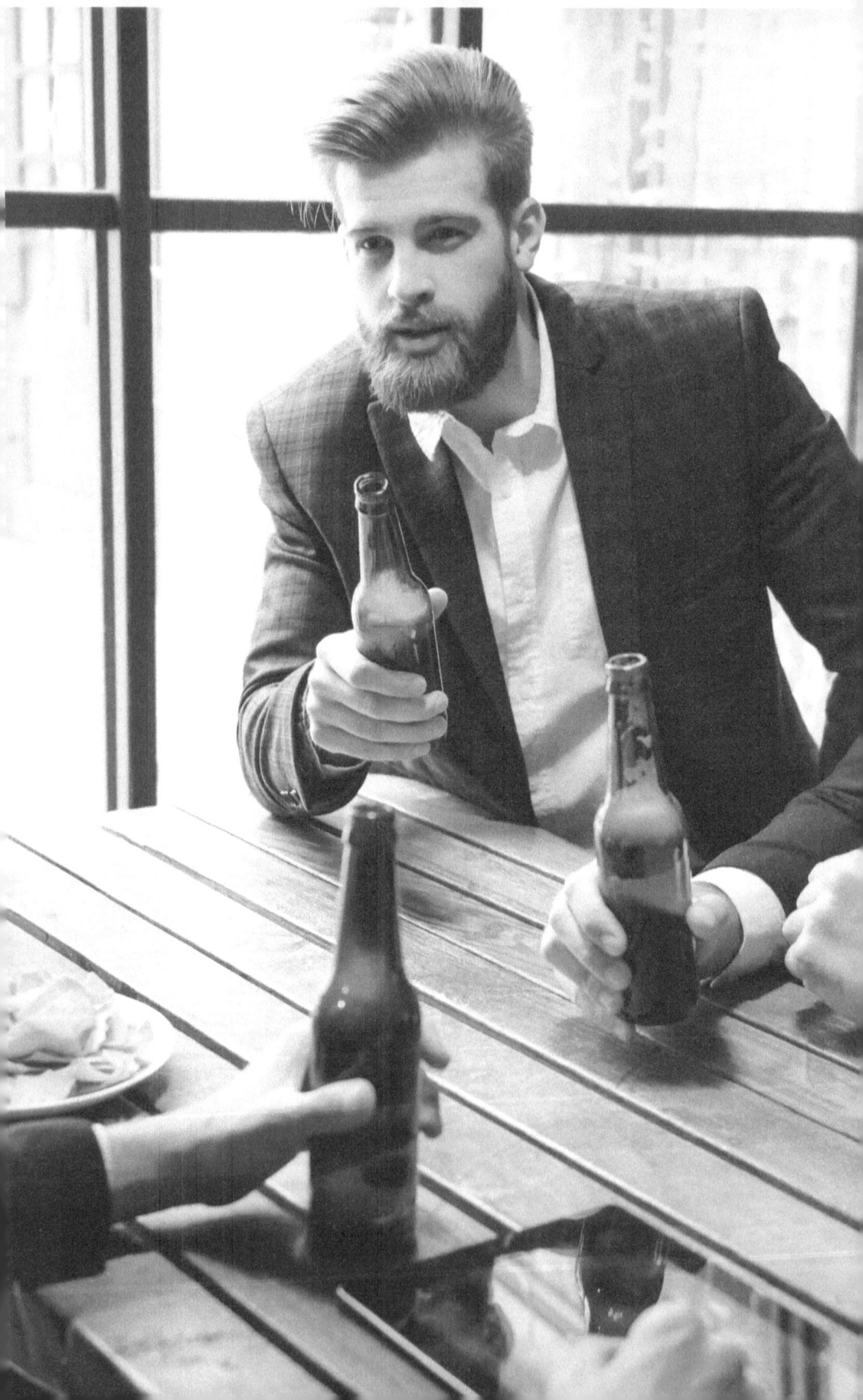

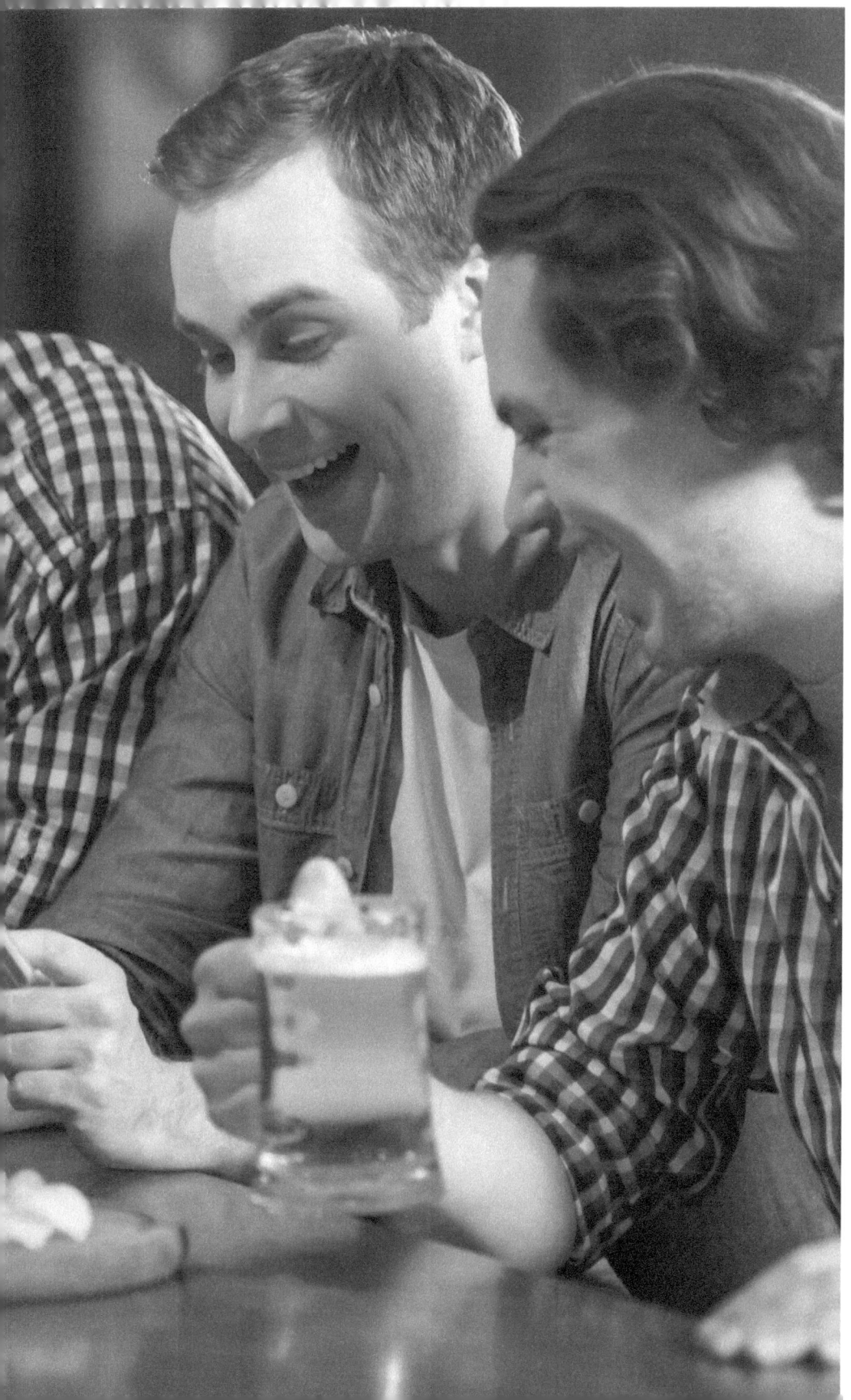

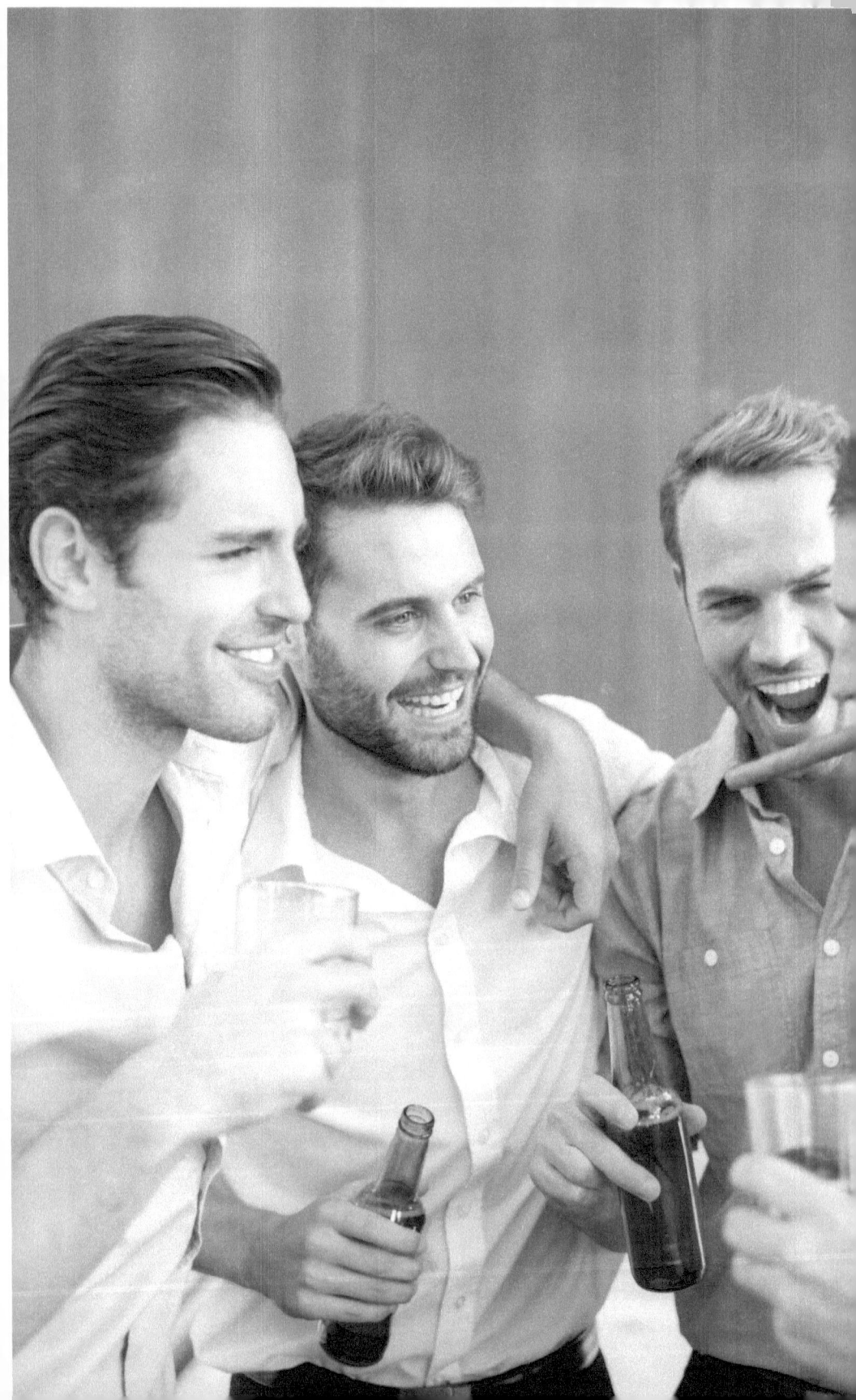

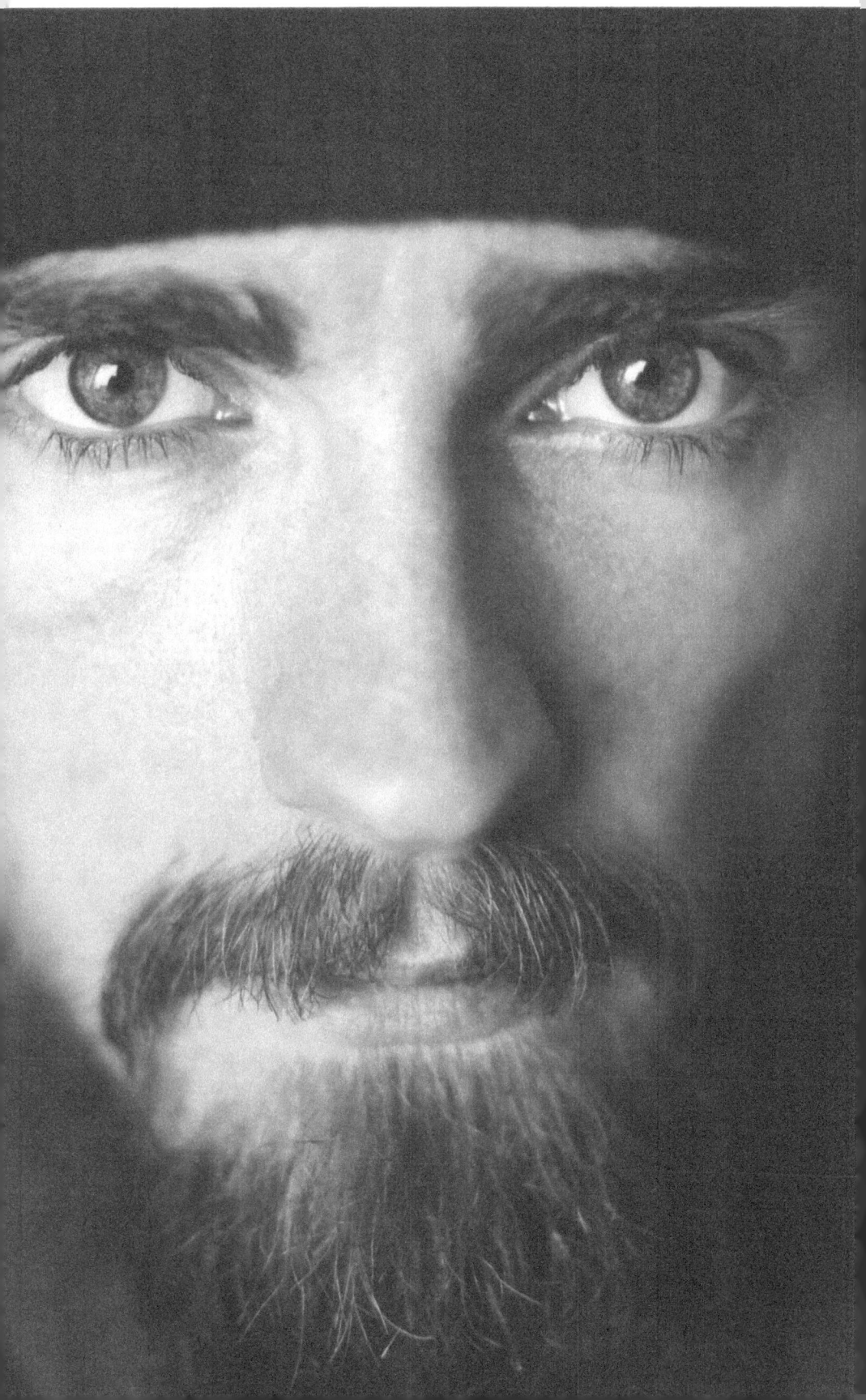

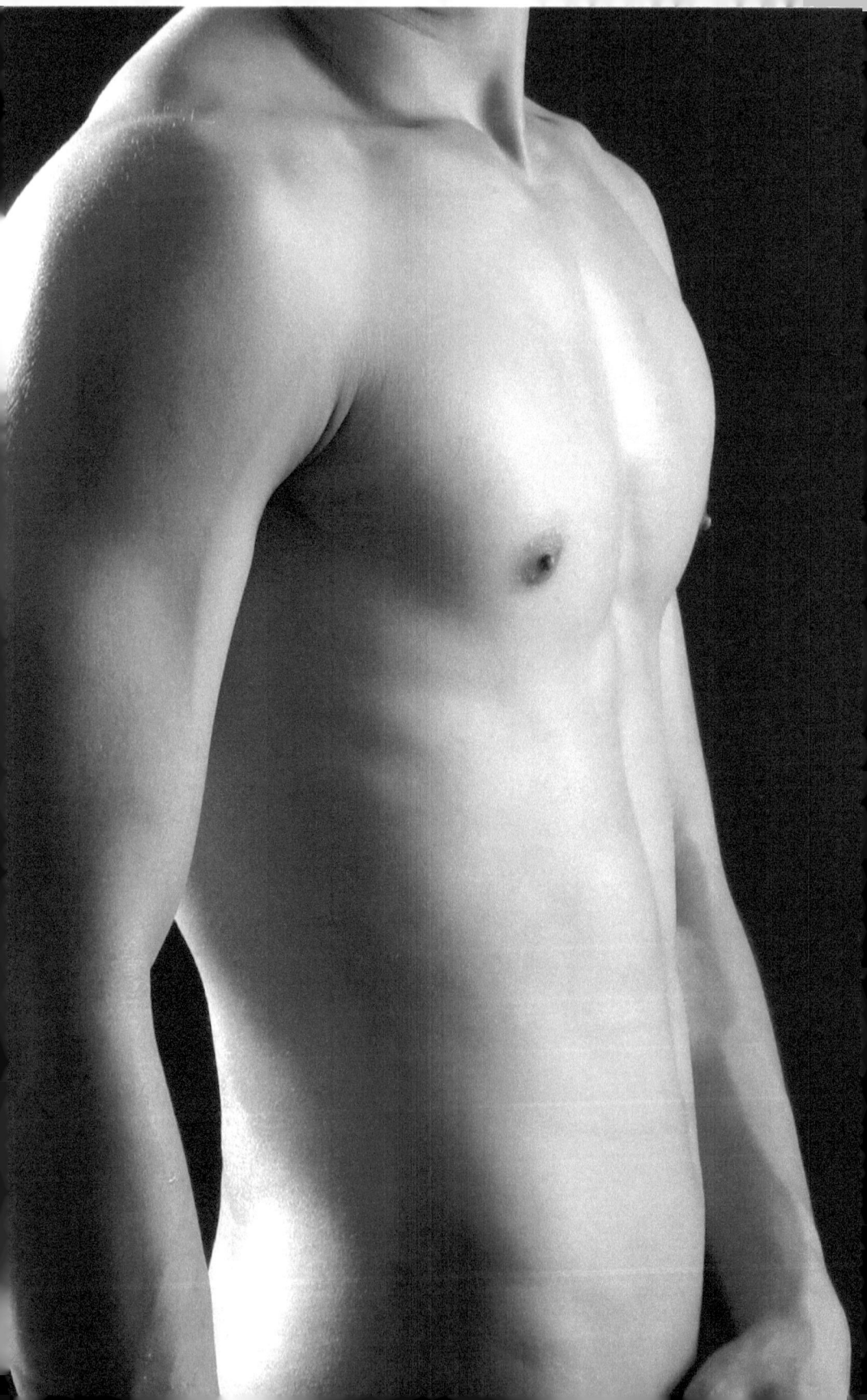

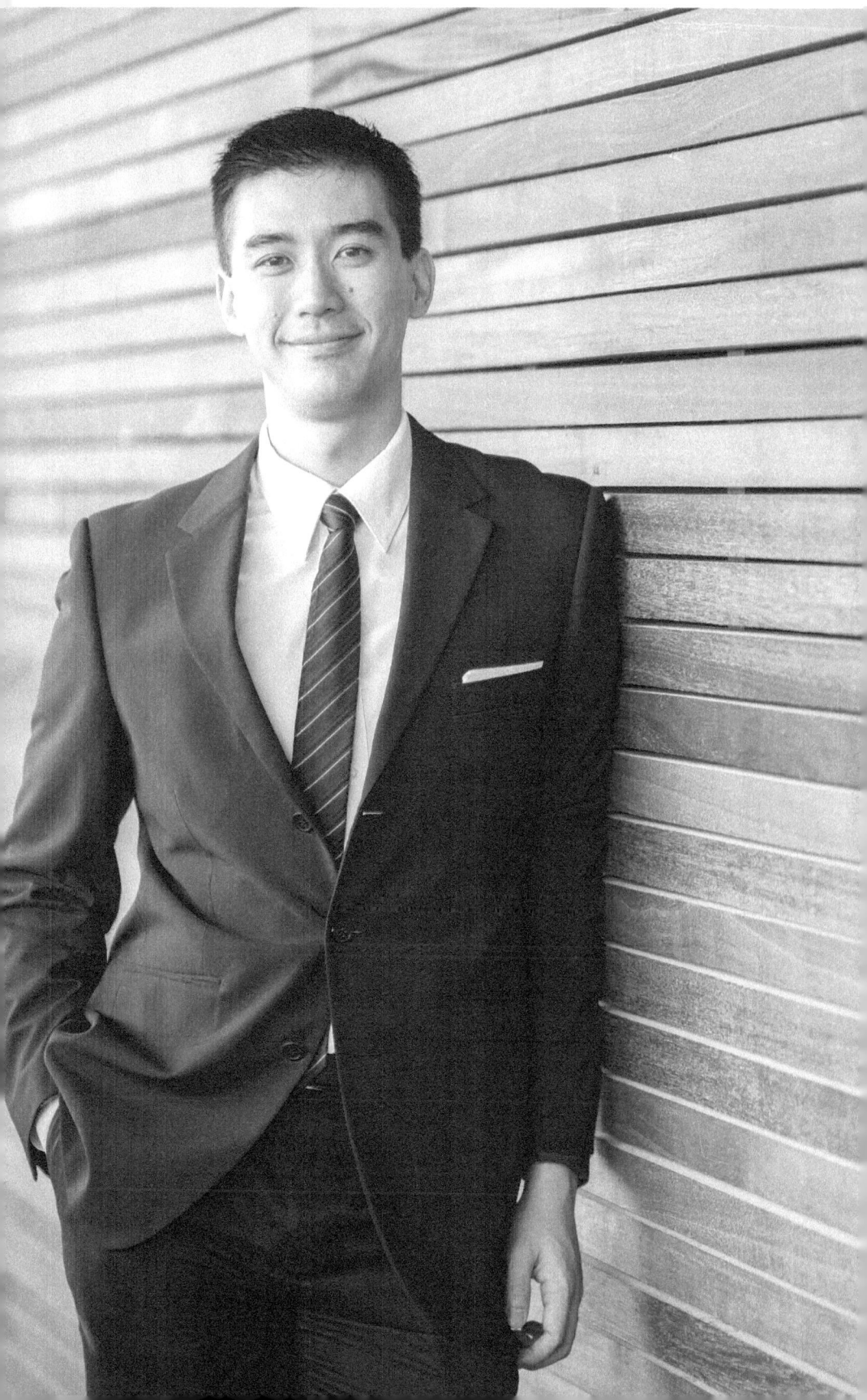

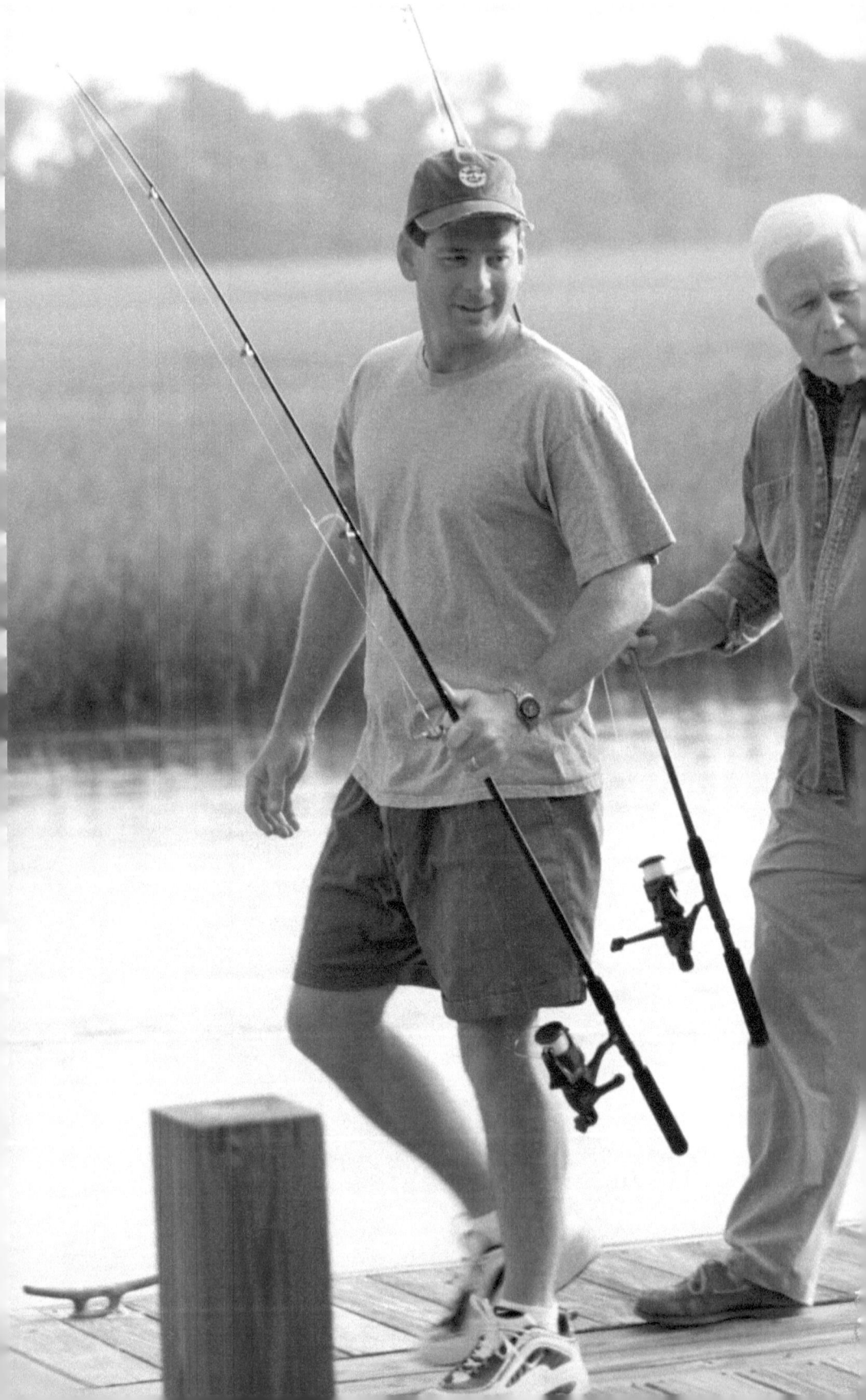

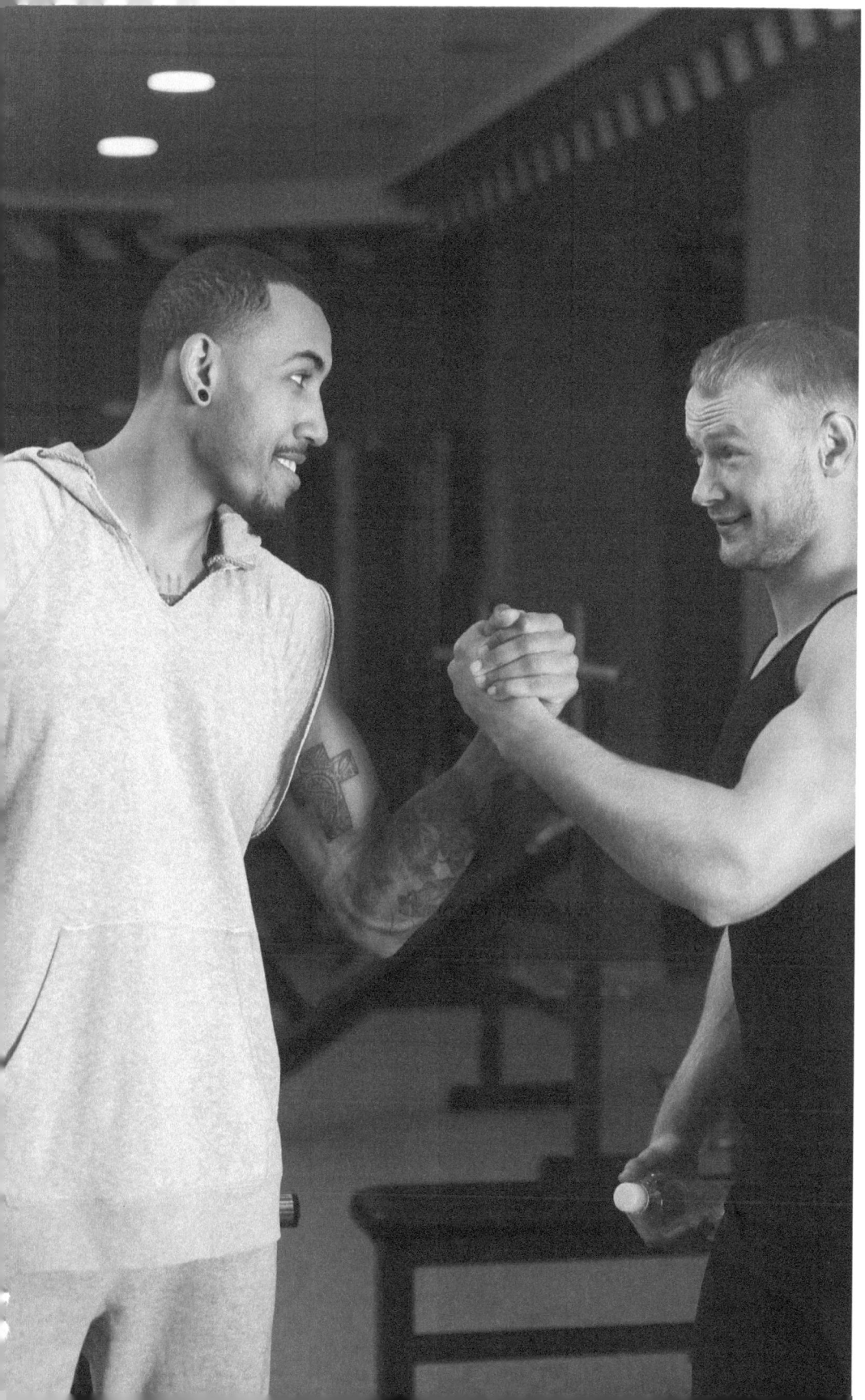

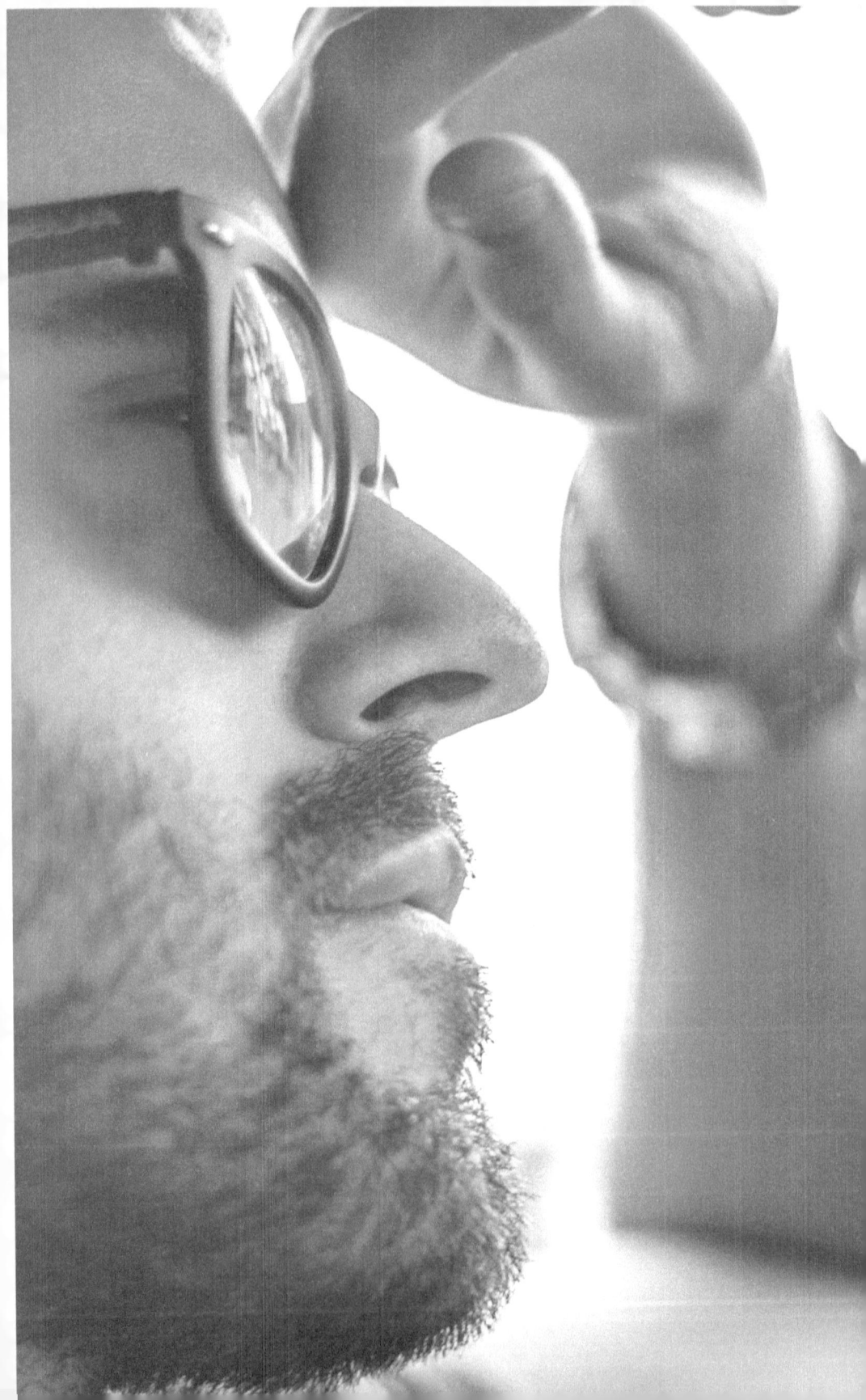

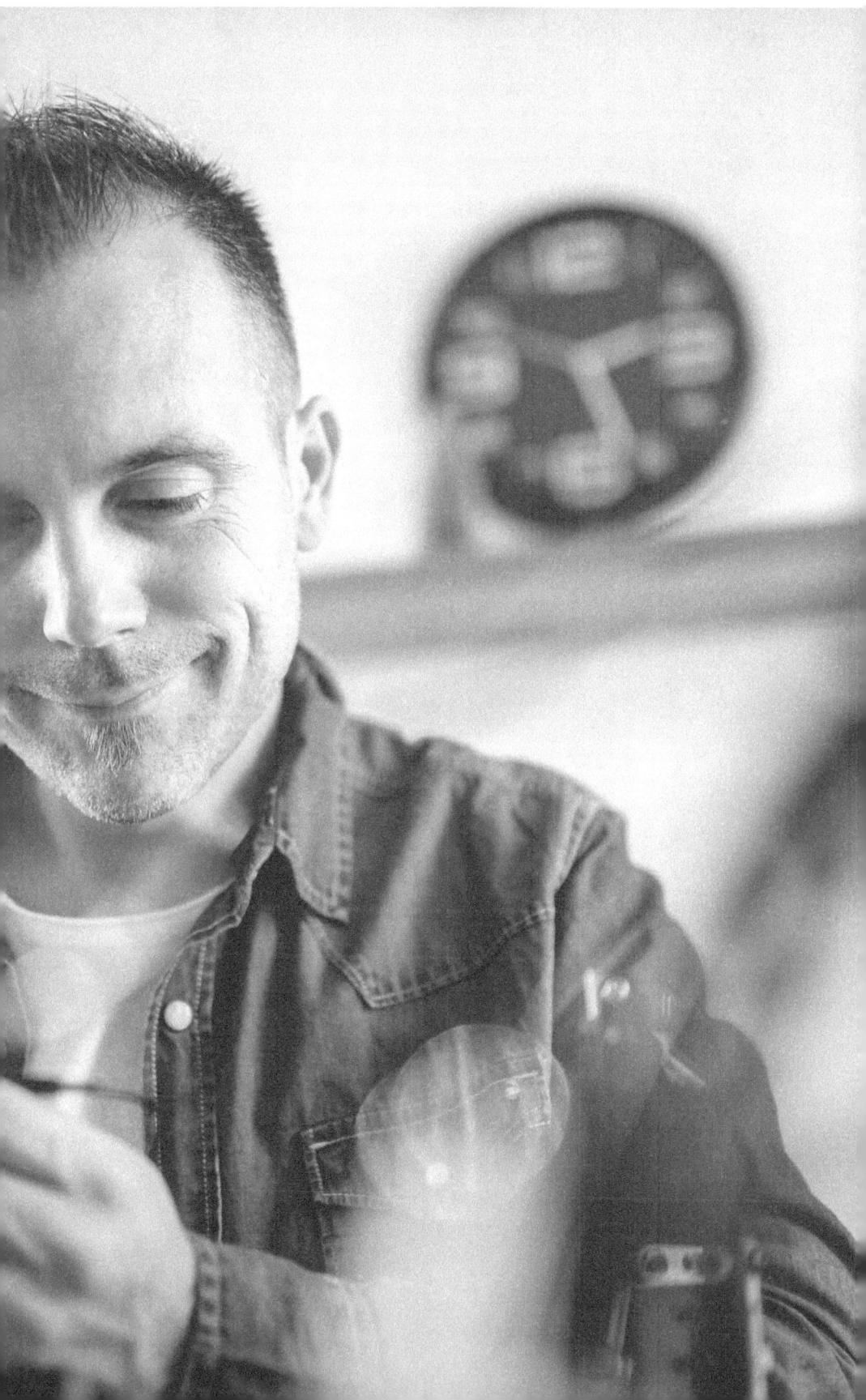

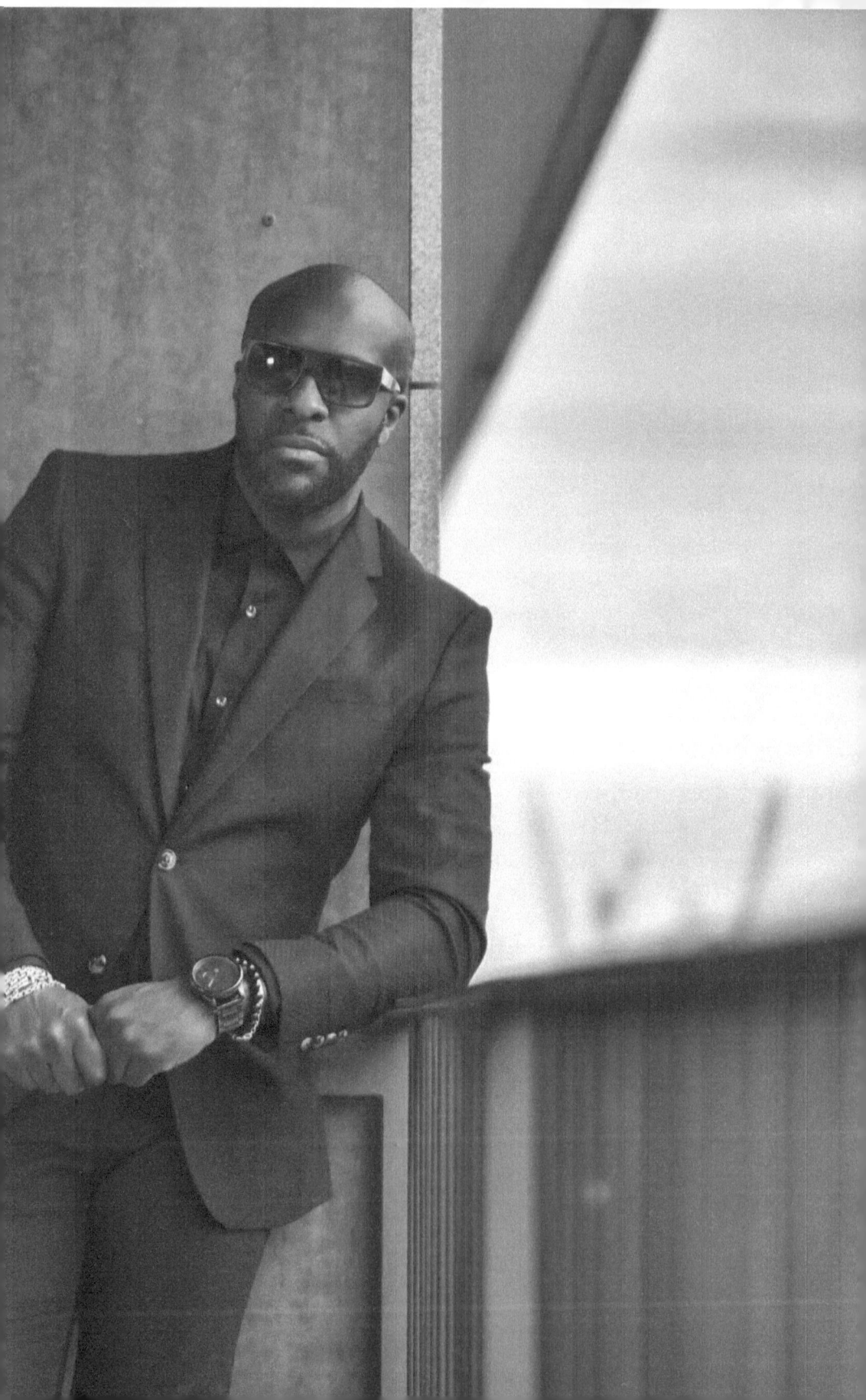

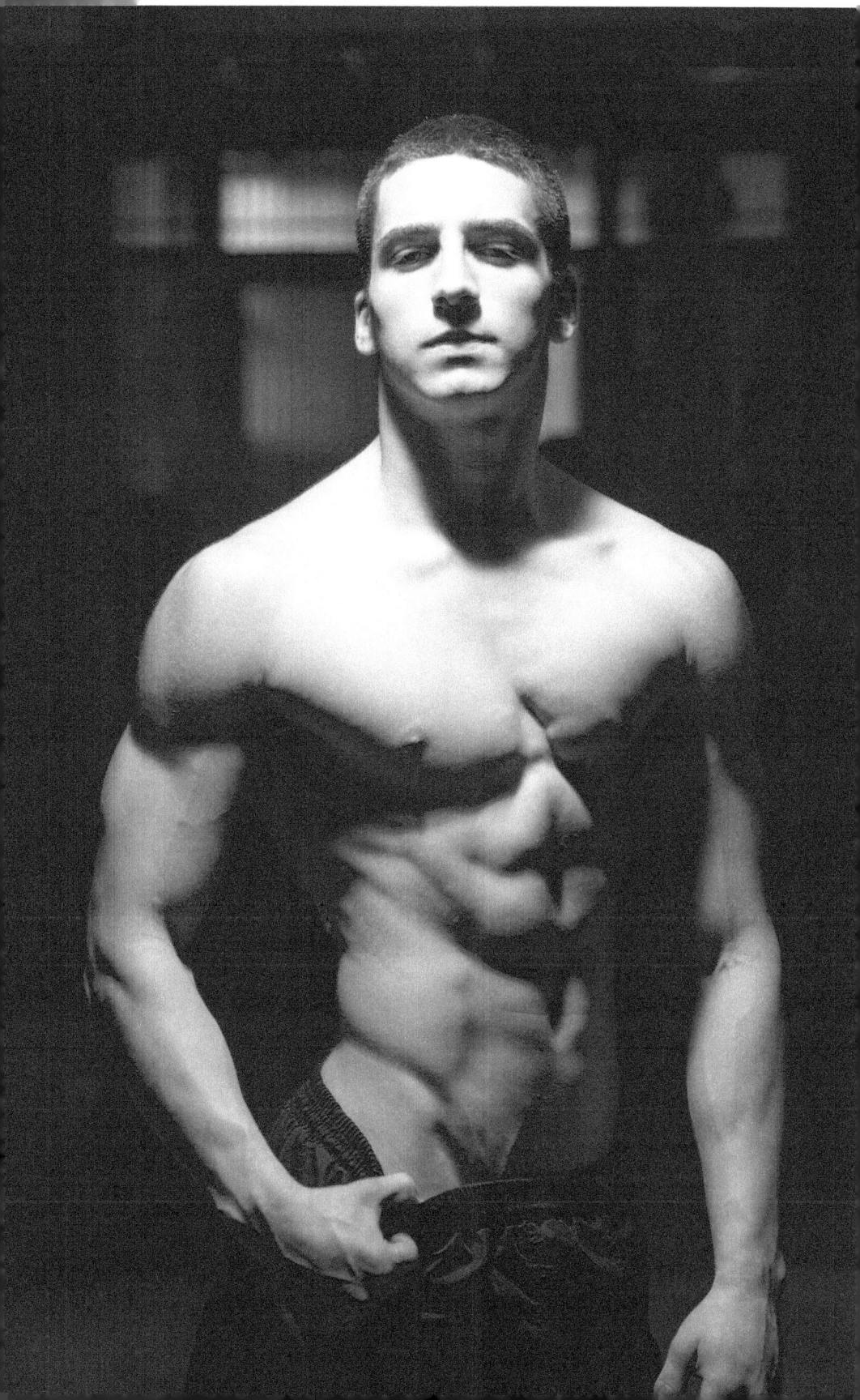

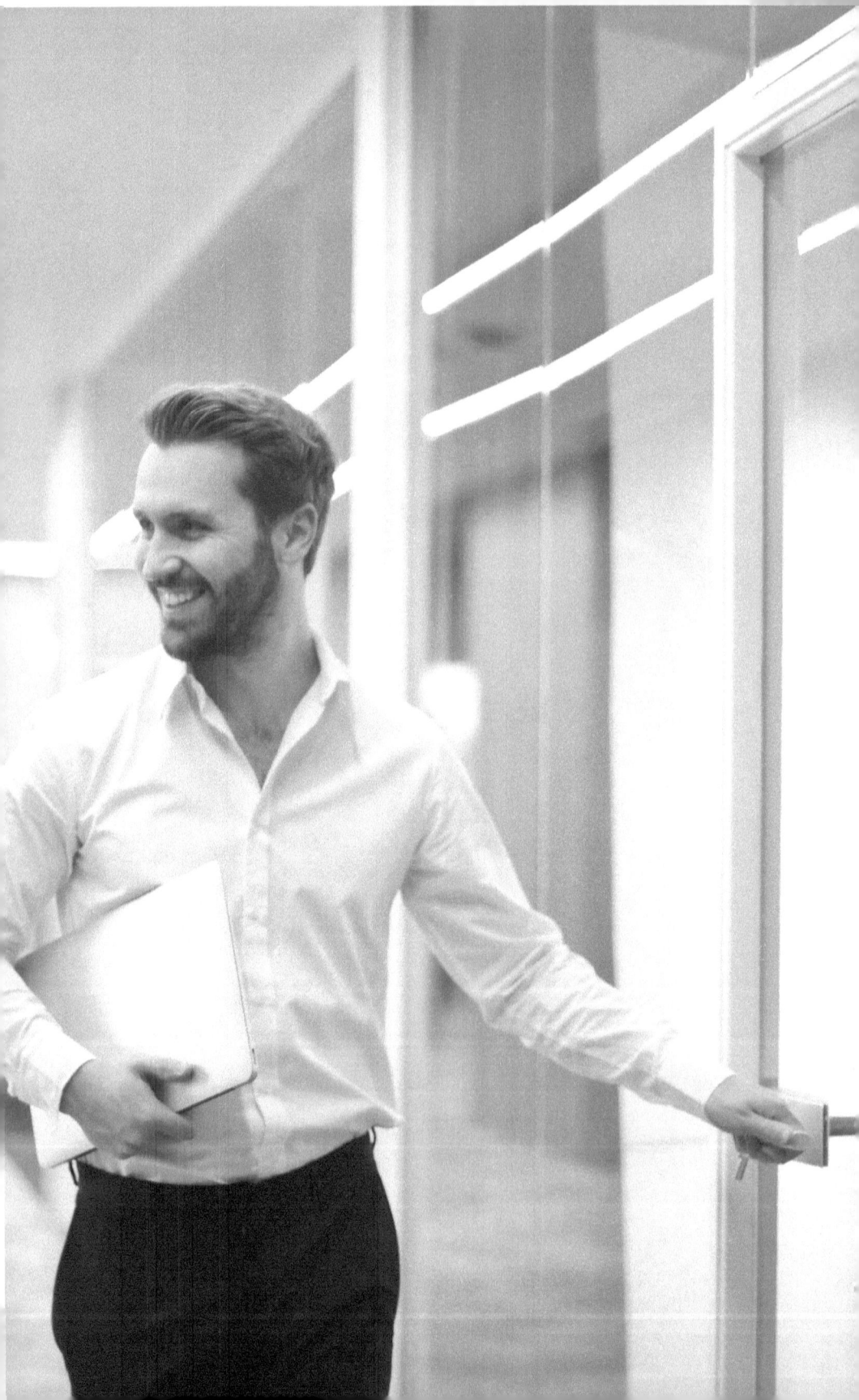

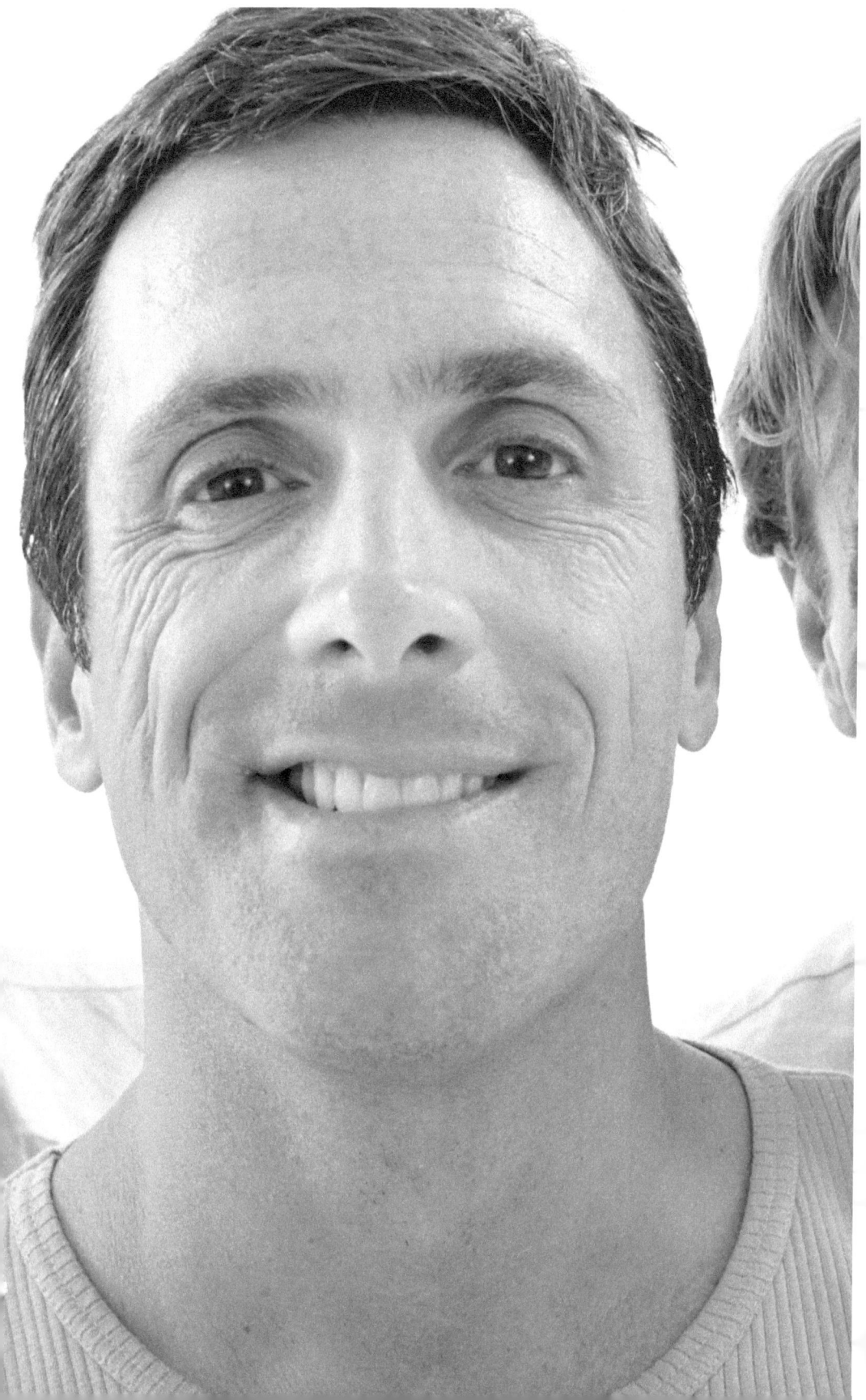

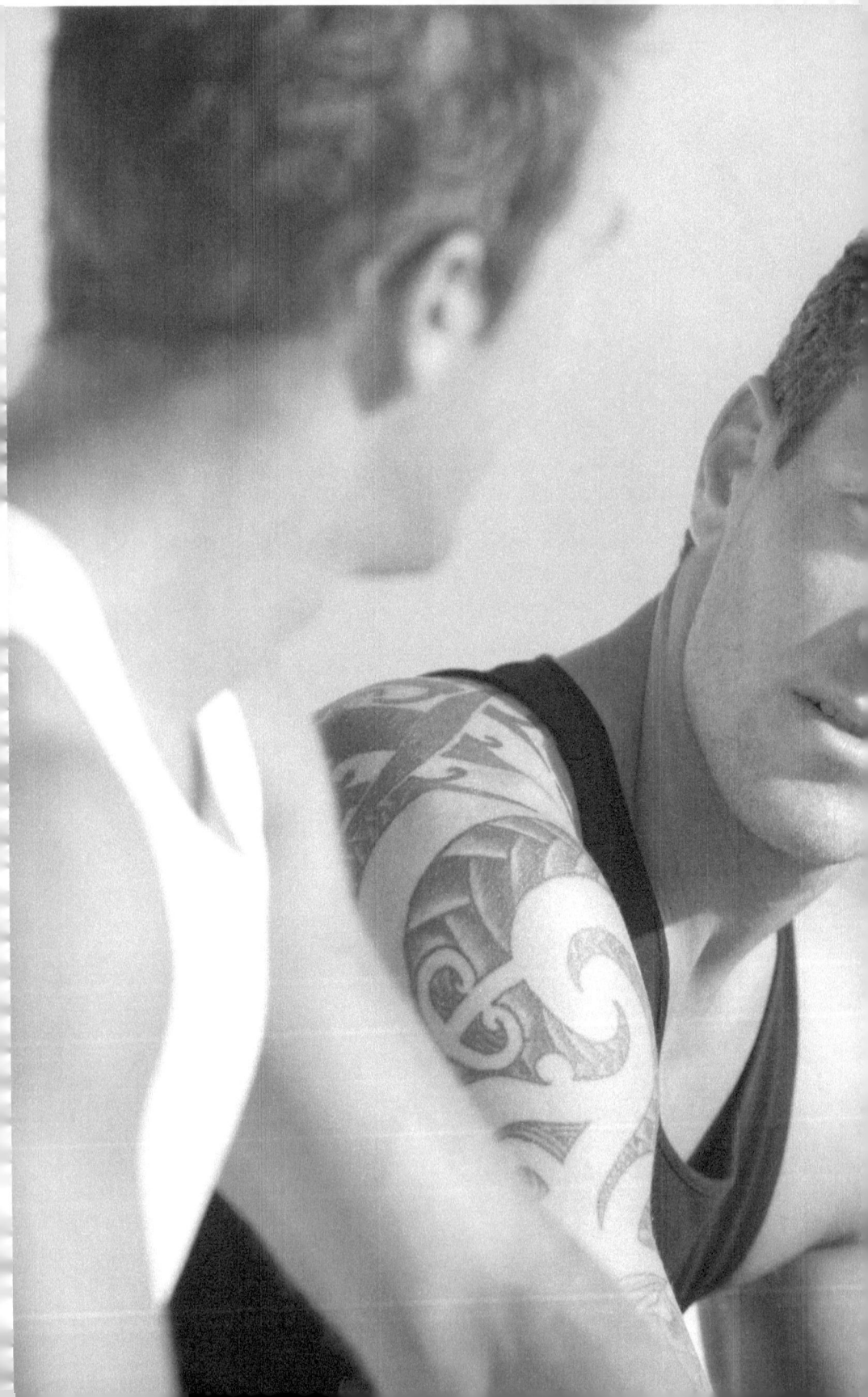

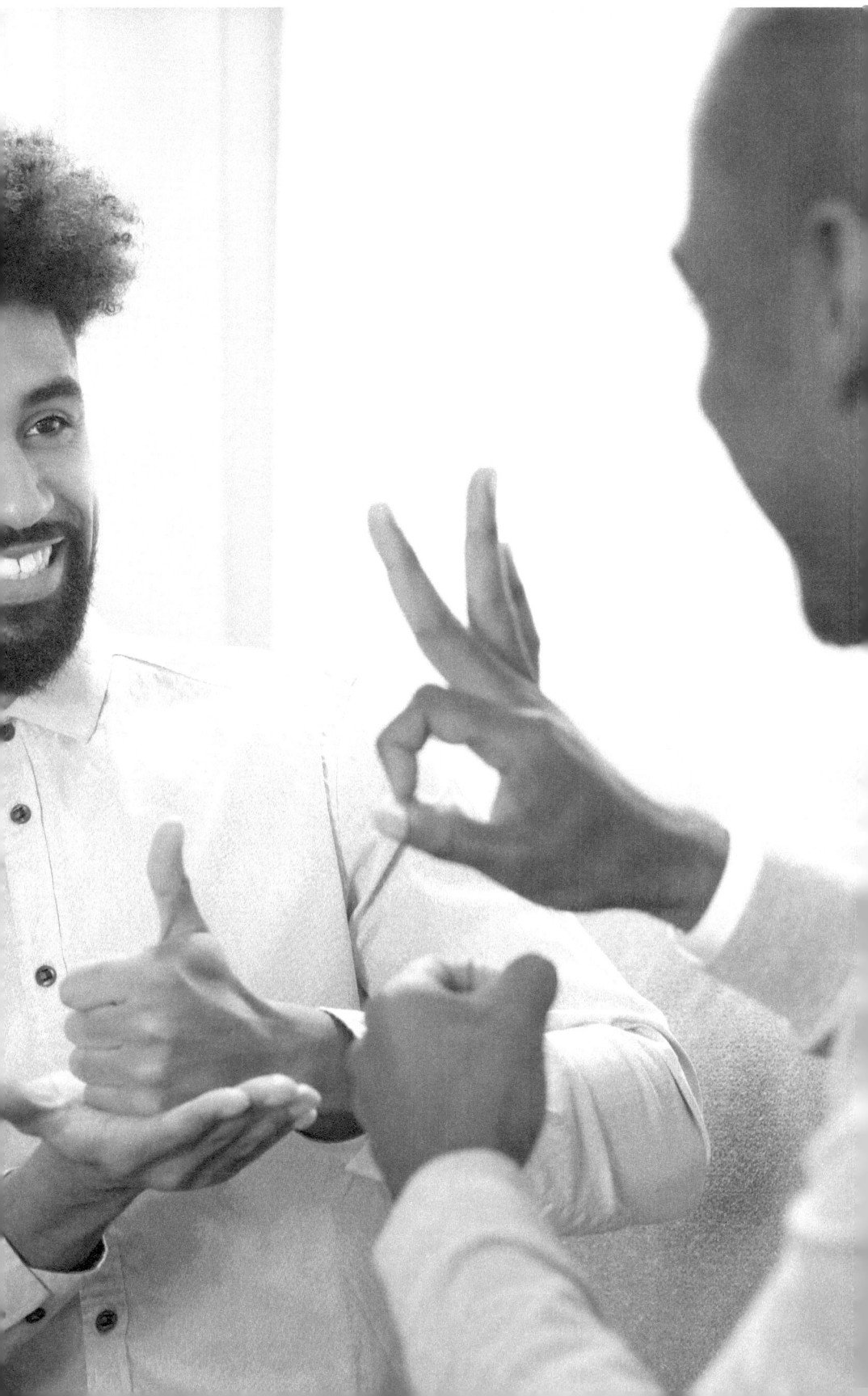

www.ingramcontent.com/pod-product-compliance
Lightning Source LLC
Chambersburg PA
CBHW021502210526
45463CB00002B/849